T0330947

ROUTLEDGE LIBRARY EDITIONS:
INTERNATIONAL SECURITY STUDIES

Volume 23

WEAPONS OF MASS DESTRUCTION AND THE ENVIRONMENT

WEAPONS OF MASS DESTRUCTION AND THE ENVIRONMENT

SIPRI
STOCKHOLM INTERNATIONAL PEACE
RESEARCH INSTITUTE

Routledge
Taylor & Francis Group

LONDON AND NEW YORK

First published in 1977 by Taylor & Francis Ltd., London

This edition first published in 2021
by Routledge
2 Park Square, Milton Park, Abingdon, Oxon OX14 4RN

and by Routledge
52 Vanderbilt Avenue, New York, NY 10017

Routledge is an imprint of the Taylor & Francis Group, an informa business

© 1977 SIPRI

All rights reserved. No part of this book may be reprinted or reproduced or utilised in any form or by any electronic, mechanical, or other means, now known or hereafter invented, including photocopying and recording, or in any information storage or retrieval system, without permission in writing from the publishers.

Trademark notice: Product or corporate names may be trademarks or registered trademarks, and are used only for identification and explanation without intent to infringe.

British Library Cataloguing in Publication Data
A catalogue record for this book is available from the British Library

ISBN: 978-0-367-68499-0 (Set)
ISBN: 978-1-00-316169-1 (Set) (ebk)
ISBN: 978-0-367-71624-0 (Volume 23) (hbk)
ISBN: 978-0-367-71630-1 (Volume 23) (pbk)
ISBN: 978-1-00-315297-2 (Volume 23) (ebk)

Publisher's Note
The publisher has gone to great lengths to ensure the quality of this reprint but points out that some imperfections in the original copies may be apparent.

Disclaimer
The publisher has made every effort to trace copyright holders and would welcome correspondence from those they have been unable to trace.

Weapons of
Mass Destruction
and the Environment

sipri

Stockholm International Peace Research Institute

Taylor & Francis Ltd
London
1977

Crane, Russak & Company, Inc.
New York

First published 1977 by Taylor & Francis Ltd., London
and Crane, Russak & Company, Inc., New York

Copyright © 1977 by SIPRI
Sveavägen 166, S-113 46 Stockholm

All rights reserved. No part of this publication may be
reproduced, stored in a retrieval system or transmitted,
in any form or by any means, electronic,
mechanical, photocopying, recording or otherwise,
without the prior permission of the copyright owner.

ISBN 0 8448 1295 1

Library of Congress Catalog Card Number 77-15308

Printed and bound in the United Kingdom by
Taylor & Francis (Printers) Ltd, Rankine Road,
Basingstoke, Hampshire RG24 0PR

Preface

Given the present state of the world, it is essential to the future well-being of mankind that nuclear, chemical, biological and other weapons of mass destruction be eliminated from the arsenals of the world. A substantial fraction of the research effort of SIPRI has been devoted to providing objective information that would help to create an appropriate climate for relevant disarmament efforts and that would also prove useful to the negotiators themselves.

The present book is the product of one of the several recent and current SIPRI projects devoted to the environmental aspects of arms control and disarmament, a hitherto neglected area of concern in this context. A partial listing of related SIPRI publications will be found on page 88. It is hoped that these documents will contribute to the success of the special session on disarmament of the UN General Assembly scheduled for May–June 1978.

This book was written by Dr Arthur H. Westing, a senior research fellow at SIPRI. He is on leave from Windham College in Putney, Vermont, where he is professor of botany.

July 1977   *Frank Barnaby*
                                                                             Director

Contents

Tables

Conventions and units of measure

As far as possible, the names of plants conform to Lawrence (1951), of the mammals to Walker *et al.* (1964), of the bacteria to Buchanan *et al.* (1974), and of the protozoa to Kudo (1966). The chemical nomenclature follows that of Stecher *et al.* (1968) or, secondarily, of Weast (1974: B–C). All units of measure follow the *Système Internationale d'Unités* (SI) (Page and Vigoureux, 1974); conversions to customary US and British units are from Weast (1974: F:282–304).

References to publications in the text provide information sufficient to locate the full bibliographic citation in the alphabetical listing of 'References', that is, author and date. Different publications by the same author that were published during the same year are distinguished by the arbitrary assignment of a series of lower case letters appended to the year of publication. Additional numbers are in some instances provided in the text immediately following the year of publication (being separated from it by a colon). These refer to specific portions or locations within the publication. Roman numerals signify chapters and Arabic numerals signify pages.

The units of measure used in the text follow:

a   = are = 10^2 square metres = 1076.39 square feet

d   = day = 86 400 seconds

°C   = degree Celsius (to obtain temperature in degrees Fahrenheit, multiply by 1.8 and then add 32)

Ci   = curie = 37×10^9 disintegrations per second = 2.22×10^{12} disintegrations per minute (dpm)

g   = gram = 10^{-3} kilogram = $2.204\,62 \times 10^{-3}$ pound

g/kt   = gram per kilotonne = 0.002 pound per 10^3 US (short) tons

g/m^3 = gram per cubic metre = $8.345\,40 \times 10^{-6}$ pound per US gallon = $10.022\,4 \times 10^{-6}$ pound per British gallon

h   = hour = 3600 seconds

h-   = hecto- = $10^2 \times$

ha   = hectare = 10^4 square metres = 10^{-2} square kilometre = 2.471 05 acres

J   = joule = 0.238 846 calorie

J/kg   = joule per kilogram = 0.108 339 calorie per pound

k-   = kilo- = $10^3 \times$

kCi   = kilocurie = 37×10^{12} disintegrations per second

kCi/kg = kilocurie per kilogram = 453.592 4 curies per pound

kCi/kt = kilocurie per kilotonne = 907.184 7 curies per 10^3 US (short) tons

kCi/Mt	= kilocurie per megatonne = 907.184 7 curies per 10^6 US (short) tons
kg	= kilogram = 2.204 62 pounds
kg/ha	= kilogram per hectare = 0.892 179 pound per acre
kg/kt	= kilogram per kilotonne = 2 pounds per 10^3 US (short) tons
kg/m^3	= kilogram per cubic metre = $8.345\ 40 \times 10^{-3}$ pound per US gallon = $10.022\ 4 \times 10^{-3}$ pound per British gallon = 1.685 55 pounds per cubic yard
kJ	= kilojoule = 10^3 joules = 238.846 calories
kJ/m^2	= kilojoule per square metre = 238.846 calories per square metre = 0.154 094 calorie per square inch
km	= kilometre = 10^3 metres = 0.621 371 mile
kPa	= kilopascal = $9.869\ 23 \times 10^{-3}$ atmosphere = 0.145 038 pound per square inch
kR	= kiloröntgen = 10^3 röntgens, which see
ks	= kilosecond = 10^3 seconds = 16.666 7 minutes
kt	= kilotonne = 10^6 kilograms = 1102.31 US (short) tons = 984.207 British (long) tons. See also Chapter 1, note 2
m	= metre = 3.280 84 feet
m-	= milli- = $10^{-3} \times$
m^2	= square metre = 10.763 9 square feet = 1550.00 square inches
m^3	= cubic metre = 10^3 litres = 264.172 US gallons = 219.969 British gallons = 1.307 95 cubic yards
m^3/ha	= cubic metre per hectare = 55.846 6 board feet per acre
mg	= milligram = 10^{-6} kilogram = $2.204\ 62 \times 10^{-6}$ pound
mg/m^3	= milligram per cubic metre = $8.345\ 40 \times 10^{-9}$ pound per US gallon = $10.022\ 4 \times 10^{-9}$ pound per British gallon
min	= minute = 60 seconds
mol	= mole = that amount of substance which contains as many elementary entities as there are atoms in 12 grams of ^{12}C, that is, 602.252×10^{21} elementary entities
mm	= millimetre = 10^{-3} metre = 0.039 370 1 inch
mmol	= millimole = 10^{-3} mole, which see
m/s	= metre per second = 3.6 kilometres per hour = 2.236 94 miles per hour
M-	= mega- = $10^6 \times$
MCi	= megacurie = 37×10^{15} disintegrations per second
MCi/kg	= megacurie per kilogram = 453.592 4 kilocuries per pound
MCi/kt	= megacurie per kilotonne = 907.184 7 kilocuries per 10^3 US (short) tons

MCi/Mt = megacurie per megatonne = 907.184 7 kilocuries per 10^6 US (short) tons

Ms = megasecond = 10^6 seconds = 11.574 1 days

Mt = megatonne = 10^9 kilograms = 1.102 31 × 10^6 US (short) tons = 0.984 207 × 10^6 British (long) ton. See also chapter 1, note 2.

μ = micro- = 10^{-6} ×

μg = microgram = 10^{-9} kilogram = 2.204 62 × 10^{-12} pound

μg/kg = microgram per kilogram = part per 10^9 parts, by weight

μg/m³ = microgram per cubic metre = 1.685 55 × 10^{-12} pound per cubic yard

n- = nano- = 10^{-9} ×

nm = nanometre = 10^{-9} metre = 39.370 1 × 10^{-9} inch = 10 Ångströms

Pa = pascal = 9.869 23 × 10^{-6} atmosphere = 145.038 × 10^{-6} pound per square inch

R = röntgen = a unit of X or gamma radiation exposure producing a charge of 258 × 10^{-6} coulomb per kilogram of air; for biota it is numerically equivalent to *ca.* 1 'rad', a unit of ionizing radiation absorption of 10^{-2} joule per kilogram of body weight (Arena, 1971: 215–218)

s = second

t = tonne = 10^3 kilograms = 1.102 31 US (short) tons = 0.984 207 British (long) ton

Foreword

The arms race between the USA and the USSR continues unabated. This unholy race is spreading ever more widely and rapidly among the other nations of the world. These two powers each maintain enormous nuclear arsenals plus the systems to deliver them. Four further nations have a demonstrated nuclear capability and several others probably have similar capabilities. Substantial numbers of nations have the chemical and microbiological expertise and production facilities to suggest that they could be maintaining chemical and biological arsenals. And a number of additional weapons of mass destruction could be available to certain nations in special locations or circumstances.

The inhumane aspects of weapons of mass destruction are widely recognized and underlie the continuing efforts in many quarters to abolish or restrict their use. Their impact on the environment, usually an ancillary aspect of their employment, has, on the other hand, been of much less general concern or interest. This is regrettable. Whereas concern for ecological disruption during warfare may to some appear misdirected or even callous, especially when such disruption appears to be in partial substitution for human destruction, it can be justified on a number of grounds. First, it is in the long-run self-interest of the human race to protect the natural environment from which it ultimately derives its sustenance. Second, all living things deserve a measure of respect and protection in their own right. Third, an exposition of the environmental damage associated with weapons of mass destruction might serve to bolster the argument to control their use, especially so in the light of today's growing environmental awareness. And fourth, a concern over ecological consequences of war does not preclude the direct traditional human concerns. It may, in fact, enhance such concerns via a civilizing influence and also perhaps by awakening a wider public to war-related concerns.

1. Nuclear weapons

Superior numerals, thus [5], *refer to notes on pages 24–30.*

I. Introduction

Nuclear weapons exist, they have been employed and they can have a tremendous ecological impact. No treatment of the interaction between weapons of mass destruction and the environment would be complete without an examination of nuclear weapons.[1]

Nuclear weapons come in all sizes or yields[2] and can be delivered in a variety of ways. The bomb that destroyed Hiroshima had an energy yield of about 13 kt and the one which destroyed Nagasaki a yield of about 21 kt (US Atomic Energy Commission, priv. comm., 9 Jan. 1974; see also Penney *et al.*, 1970). Although a nuclear device of over 50 Mt has been detonated (Glasstone, 1964: 681 a), one gathers that likely sizes for use as strategic nuclear weapons would be in the range of 1 Mt to 10 Mt. Hundreds if not thousands of such weapons might be expended within a period of days during some major nuclear exchange of the future. By way of partial contrast, the total energy yield of all the munitions expended during $8\frac{1}{2}$ years of the Second Indochina War comes to less than 4 Mt (note 3).

Nuclear weapons are awe-inspiring not only for their total energy yield, but also for the several forms in which this energy is dissipated, as will be seen in the following section. The ecological consequences of nuclear war are covered in section III of this chapter.

II. Description

General

The effects of a nuclear attack depend not only upon the number of devices detonated and their types and sizes, but also upon how they are distributed in time and space. The effects are strongly influenced by whether a burst occurs at or near ground level, substantially below ground, under water, in the denser portions of the atmosphere (that is, below about 30 km), or even in the very rarified upper atmosphere.[4]

The character of the terrain, weather conditions and other factors also modify the character and magnitude of the effects.

A nuclear bomb that bursts in the troposphere high enough that its fire-ball does not reach the ground[5] will dissipate about half of its energy in the form of a blast or shock wave (Table 1.1). Another third of the energy will be released in the form of thermal radiation. The remaining energy will be expended in the form of nuclear radiation, about one third of this within the initial minute and the rest over a much longer period of time.

A burst in the very thin air above the stratosphere[4] will translate significantly less of its energy into blast and more into thermal radiation. Surface and sub-surface bursts, either terrestrial or aquatic, produce far more radioactive fall-out than do air bursts. Underwater bursts are a class by themselves. Their effects differ markedly depending upon how far below the surface the bomb is detonated, how deep and how large the body of water is and other factors. The reader is referred to Glasstone (1964: VI) for further information on underwater nuclear explosions.

In the sections that follow can be found separate descriptions of the blast (shock) wave of a nuclear detonation, of its pulse of thermal radiation and of its nuclear radiation. The tabulated data are usually presented for three bomb sizes: 18 kt, 0.91 Mt and 9.1 Mt (note 2). The smallest of these is roughly comparable to the Hiroshima and Nagasaki shots, whereas the larger two sizes are likely to be employed in any future nuclear war.

The ecological consequences of nuclear attack will in many respects be similar to those of conventional warfare or other major environmental disturbance. The consequences will differ, however, owing to the novel stresses imposed upon the involved ecosystems by nuclear (and perhaps also ultra-violet) radiation. And, depending upon the magnitude of the nuclear exchange, they can differ dramatically in scale.

Blast (shock) wave

Within seconds of detonation, a nuclear bomb dissipates about half of its tremendous energy in the form of a blast or shock wave (Table 1.1). This wave, which initially propagates outward at many times the speed of sound (and eventually turns into a sound wave), is responsible for much of the physical damage brought about by a nuclear explosion. Since the parameters of a blast wave are highly complex even under idealized conditions, the data on damage presented below are based largely on empirically gathered information (Glasstone, 1964: III–V).

Table 1.1. Distribution of energy release by a nuclear bomb exploded in the troposphere

Energy form		Energy released		
		$(10^{12}$ J)	$(10^{15}$ J)	$(10^{15}$ J)
	Bomb size:	18 kt	0.91 Mt	9.1 Mt
Blast (shock)		41.9	2.28	22.8
Thermal radiation		29.3	1.59	15.9
Nuclear radiation, first min		4.2	0.10	1.0
Nuclear radiation, residual		8.4	0.21	2.1
Total		**83.7**	**4.19**	**41.9**

Notes:

(a) For an explanation of bomb size designations, see note 2.

(b) The data are derived from those of Glasstone (1964: 7-9).

(c) The 18 kt bomb is a fission bomb, whereas the 0.91 Mt and 9.1 Mt bombs are half fission and half fusion. The explosions are so-called typical air bursts.[5] Comparable data for surface bursts are difficult to generalize about.

Table 1.2. Blast damage to forests from a nuclear bomb exploded in the troposphere

Level of damage		Size of damaged area		
	Bomb size:	18 kt	0.91 Mt	9.1 Mt
30 % Blowdown				
Diameter (km)		4.0	18.3	46.9
Area (ha)		1 270	26 300	173 000
90 % Blowdown				
Diameter (km)		2.7	13.4	32.3
Area (ha)		565	14 100	82 000

Notes:

(a) For an explanation of bomb size designations, see note 2.

(b) The data are derived from those of Glasstone (1964: 169, 174-175). They compare well with those of Fons et al. (1957).

(c) The data refer to what was described as an 'average' coniferous forest growing under 'unfavourable' conditions, but were asserted to be equally applicable to a dicotyledonous forest in leaf.

(d) To bring about equal damage by a steady wind would require a velocity of 40-45 m/s to blow down 30 per cent of the trees and 58-63 m/s to blow down 90 per cent. These steady wind velocities are roughly comparable to the transient ones at the shock front which can be theoretically derived for the distances involved (Glasstone, 1964: 107, 135).

(e) The explosions are so-called typical air bursts.[5] Comparable data for surface bursts would have diameters roughly 80 per cent and areas 64 per cent of those presented (Glasstone, 1964: 632, 107).

4

With respect to trees, the destructive force of a blast wave from a nuclear detonation is best related to the peak transient wind (or particle) velocity at the shock front. The effect (known as drag loading) caused by this transient wind is more destructive than one might expect from a knowledge of blast waves initiated by conventional explosives, because of its relatively long duration. The greater the distance from the explosion, the longer is the duration of this positive phase, varying from roughly 0·5 s to 1 s for an 18 kt bomb, from 2 s to 4 s for a 0.91 Mt bomb and from 4 s to 8 s for a 9.1 Mt bomb. Thus the increasing duration with distance compensates in part for the decreasing velocity of the peak transient wind. A 0.91 Mt bomb will blow down most of the trees on 14×10^3 ha if it is an air burst, or on 9×10^3 ha if a surface burst (Table 1.2).

With respect to wildlife, the destructive force of a blast wave from a nuclear detonation is best related to the peak transient overpressure at the shock front, that is, the transient maximum pressure above atmospheric. Significant damage can occur to the lungs of large mammals (including humans) at a point where the nuclear blast wave, with its lengthy positive phase, has a peak transient overpressure of about 100 kPa (Glasstone, 1964: 557). Approximately 1 per cent of such

Table 1.3. **Blast damage to wildlife from a nuclear bomb exploded in the troposphere**

	Size of damaged area		
Bomb size:	18 kt	0.91 Mt	9.1 Mt
Lung damage			
Diameter (km)	1.4	5.1	10.9
Area (ha)	148	2 010	9 330
Lethal to 50 %			
Diameter (km)	0.7	2.7	5.9
Area (ha)	43	591	2 740

Notes:

(a) For an explanation of bomb size designations, see note 2.

(b) The data are derived from those of Glasstone (1964: 135). Lung damage is considered to occur at a transient overpressure of 100 kPa or more, and 50 per cent lethality at 345 kPa or more (Glasstone, 1964: 557).

(c) The above figures are based only on the incident or free-field overpressures which develop. These are, in fact, augmented by reflected overpressures which (depending upon height of burst, terrain, etc.) can more than double the total (so-called Mach front) overpressures experienced at any distance.

(d) The explosions are so-called typical air bursts.[5] Comparable data for surface bursts would have diameters roughly 75 per cent and areas 56 per cent of those presented (Glasstone, 1964: 632, 638).

exposed animals will be killed at an overpressure of 275 kPa, 50 per cent at 345 kPa and 99 per cent at 415 kPa. Through the transient overpressure it generates, a 0.91 Mt bomb will kill more than half the wildlife on about 590 ha if it is an air burst, or on 330 ha if a surface burst (Table 1.3).

It is important to note that these wildlife mortality data are based only on the incident or free-field overpressures that develop. The area of blast fatalities is, however, enlarged in a number of ways. First, the incident overpressures are augmented by reflected overpressures. And second, a very high, though variable, proportion of animal deaths and injuries is not attributable to the blast *per se* (the so-called primary blast effects), but rather to flying missiles (so-called secondary blast effects) and to body displacement, that is, to having the body slammed into some object (so-called tertiary blast effects). Depending especially on the terrain, these indirect effects on the blast wave can considerably intensify and enlarge the zone of wildlife casualties.

The shock wave of a surface or sub-surface burst will blast out an immense crater. For example, a 0.91 Mt bomb detonated at or near ground level will produce in dry soil a crater having a surface area of about 12 ha and a maximum depth of about 90 m (Table 1.4). The

Table 1.4. Size of crater produced by a nuclear bomb exploded at the surface

		Crater dimensions		
	Bomb size:	18 kt	0.91 Mt	9.1 Mt
Diameter (m)		108	396	854
Surface area (ha)		1	12	57
Maximum depth (m)		25	91	197
Volume (10^3 m^3)		75	3 760	37 600
Displaced mass (10^6 kg)		199	9 960	99 600

Notes:

(*a*) For an explanation of bomb size designations, see note 2.

(*b*) The data are derived from those of Glasstone (1964: 276–277). (See also Brode (1968: 193–198).)

(*c*) Volume is based on the assumption that crater shape is conical. Displaced mass is based on the assumption that soil and rock weigh 2650 kg/m^3 (Lutz and Chandler, 1946: 236; Daly *et al.*, 1966).

(*d*) The data presented are for explosions at or near the surface of dry soil. If the material were rock in lieu of soil, then the diameters and depths would be roughly 80 per cent of those given, the areas 64 per cent and the volumes (and masses) 51 per cent (Glasstone, 1964: 292).

(*e*) Subsurface bursts at optimal depth would, roughly speaking, double the diameters presented, quadruple the areas, triple the depths and increase the volumes (and masses) by a factor of twelve (Glasstone, 1964: 293). A so-called typical air burst[5] would not produce a crater (Glasstone, 1964: 277).

volume of such a crater is thus almost 4×10^6 m^3 in size. It is estimated that roughly 0.5 per cent of the material blown out of the crater is injected into the stratosphere for a residence time of perhaps one to three years (Nier *et al.*, 1975: 54). The implications of this contamination are discussed below.

Finally one should add that there is a remote possibility that underground nuclear detonations might trigger an earthquake or related seismic event in a location that is tectonically unstable (Bolt, 1976: X; Boucher *et al.*, 1969).

Thermal radiation

Fires are virtually certain following an above-ground nuclear detonation. This is because approximately one-third of the bomb's immense energy is dissipated during the initial several seconds after the burst as an immense pulse of thermal energy that propagates outward at almost the speed of light (Table 1.1). Under appropriate site and weather conditions, there will be large wildfires, some of which may develop into so-called mass fires or fire storms.[6]

The amount of thermal energy or radiant exposure from a nuclear bomb required to ignite vegetation varies not only with the type of

Table 1.5. **Pulse of radiant exposure required for igniting plant materials from a nuclear bomb explosion**

Plant material (dry)		Radiant exposure required for ignition (kJ/m^2)		
	Bomb size:	18 kt	0.91 Mt	9.1 Mt
Rotted conifer wood (*Abies*: Pinaceae)		150	250	330
Dicotyledonous leaves (*Fagus*: Fagaceae)		150	250	330
Grass (*Bromus*: Gramineae)		180	330	420
Sedge (*Carex*: Cyperaceae)		220	380	460
Brown conifer needles (*Pinus*: Pinaceae)		360	670	880

Notes:

(a) For an explanation of bomb size designations, see note 2.

(b) The data are derived from those of Glasstone (1964: 332).

(c) As bomb size increases, a higher level of radiant exposure is required to achieve the same effect. This is because as bomb size increases, a given amount of energy delivered to a given point in space is spread over a longer period of time (Glasstone, 1964: 571).

Table 1.6. Pulse of radiant exposure required for burn damage from a nuclear bomb explosion

	Radiation exposure required (kJ/m²)		
Bomb size:	18 kt	0.91 Mt	9.1 Mt
First-degree burn	100	130	150
Second-degree burn	180	270	380
Burns lethal to 50 %	380	590	750

Notes:

    (a) For an explanation of bomb size designations, see note 2.

    (b) The data for first-degree and second-degree burns are derived from those of Glasstone (1964: 571); the data for 50 per cent lethality are from the US Department of Defense (priv. comm., 25 Feb. 1976). (See also Defense Civil Preparedness Agency (1973: III: 2).)

    (c) The data are for flash burns of the exposed skin of pigs (*Sus*: Suidae) or humans.

    (d) As bomb size increases, a higher level of radiant exposure is required to achieve the same effect. This is because as bomb size increases, a given amount of energy delivered to a given point in space is spread over a longer period of time (Glasstone, 1964: 571).

plant material, its size and state of moisture content, but also with the duration of exposure. A given amount of radiant exposure is more effective in igniting a potential fuel if delivered in a briefer span of time. On the other hand, the larger a nuclear bomb, the more protracted is its pulse of energy. Thus, by way of example, for an 18 kt bomb to ignite dry conifer needles requires only 360 kJ/m², for a 0.91 Mt bomb the comparable value is 670 kJ/m² and for a 9.1 Mt bomb it is 880 kJ/m² (Table 1.5).

With direct injury to wildlife in mind, it can be noted that 50 per cent or more of those exposed would be burnt to death by a pulse of radiant exposure of 380 kJ/m² from an 18 kt bomb, of 590 kJ/m² from a 0.91 Mt bomb and of 750 kJ/m² from a 9.1 Mt bomb (Table 1.6). There would be additional wildlife damage from the wildfires started.

When a nuclear bomb's zone of likely ignitions (approximately that zone experiencing a radiant exposure of at least 500 kJ/m² from an 18 kt bomb, 750 kJ/m² from a 0.91 Mt bomb or 1 000 kJ/m² from a 9.1 Mt bomb) overlaps a forested region, under reasonably dry conditions the initiation of many small and several large fires is virtually certain. Depending upon the fuel and weather conditions, the burning areas within this zone could in large part coalesce during the course of the first day (Chandler *et al.*, 1963). For a 0.91 Mt bomb, this zone would on a clear day extend over some 33 × 10³ ha if it is an air burst, or over 21 × 10³ ha if a surface burst (Table 1.7), and fire might spread beyond this initial zone of ignitions, particularly if the attack occurred during the so-called fire season.

Table 1.7. Pulse of radiant exposure from a nuclear bomb exploded in the troposphere

Radiant exposure	Bomb size:	Size of area receiving more than the given radiant exposure		
		18 kt	0.91 Mt	9.1 Mt
250 kJ/m^2				
Diameter (km)		5.5	35.4	96.6
Area (ha)		2 350	98 500	732 000
500 kJ/m^2				
Diameter (km)		3·9	25.1	67.6
Area (ha)		1 170	49 500	359 000
750 kJ/m^2				
Diameter (km)		3.2	20.6	54.7
Area (ha)		781	33 300	235 000
1 000 kJ/m^2				
Diameter (km)		2.8	17.7	48.3
Area (ha)		602	24 600	183 000

Notes:

(a) For an explanation of bomb size designations, see note 2.

(b) The data are derived from those of Glasstone (1964: 333).

(c) The data presented would obtain on an unusually clear day, visibility 80 km. A reduction in visibility from 80 km to 16 km, the situation on a moderately clear day, would reduce the radiant exposures presented above to roughly 81 per cent of the values given (Glasstone, 1964: 319–320), and thus the diameters to roughly 81 per cent and the areas to 65 per cent. (For somewhat different reduction values, see the Defense Civil Preparedness Agency (1973: III: 4).)

(d) The explosions are so-called typical air bursts.[5] Comparable data for surface bursts would have diameters roughly 80 per cent and areas 64 per cent of those presented (Glasstone, 1964: 632).

(e) A given pulse of radiant exposure from a 0.91 Mt bomb is about 64 per cent as potent as one from an 18 kt bomb; the pulse of radiant exposure from a 9.1 Mt bomb is about 77 per cent as potent as one from a 0.91 Mt bomb (cf. tables 1.5 and 1.6). Thus 500 kJ/m^2 from an 18 kt bomb, 750 kJ/m^2 from a 0.91 Mt bomb and 1 000 kJ/m^2 from a 9.1 Mt are all roughly comparable in their ability to do damage.

Beyond the immediate fires that result from a nuclear detonation, there is likely to be a higher incidence of subsequent fires. This is so because, over a period of time, there will be a zone of vegetation killed by nuclear radiation that will provide an excellent source of fuel. The ecological consequences of large-scale wildfires are examined in Chapter 3.

Another effect of the exceedingly high temperatures momentarily produced by a nuclear detonation is to transform a certain fraction of the air into such oxides of nitrogen as nitric oxide (NO) and nitrogen dioxide (NO$_2$) (Bauer and Gilmore, 1975; Foley and Ruderman, 1973; Goldsmith *et al.*, 1973; Johnston *et al.*, 1973). Actually, the thermal energy that drives these reactions derives not only from the pulse of thermal radiation, but also from shock heating and bombardment by nuclear radiation. An air burst of an 18 kt bomb produces about 100×10^3 kg of these oxides of nitrogen, a 0.91 Mt bomb about 5×10^6 kg and a 9.1 Mt bomb about 50×10^6 kg. Much of this material finds its way into the lower stratosphere, where it reacts catalytically with the ozone (O_3), degrading it to oxygen gas (O_2). The implications of this effect are discussed in section III.

Nuclear radiation

Nuclear radiation represents only about 15 per cent of the total energy release of a nuclear fission bomb, and perhaps half that amount for a fission/fusion bomb (Table 1.1). About one third of the nuclear radiation released is dissipated during the first minute following detonation (Table 1.8) and thus over a relatively restricted area. Following this initial burst, the residual nuclear radiation is dissipated ever more slowly and widely. For an air burst, the radioactive contamination that occurs during the first minute (the so-called initial radiation) is the portion of substantial ecological concern. For a surface burst, this contamination is spread during roughly the first 24 hours (the so-called early radiation) owing to

Table 1.8. Dissipation of nuclear radiation from a nuclear bomb explosion

		Energy dissipated		
		$(10^{12}$ J$)$	$(10^{12}$ J$)$	$(10^{15}$ J$)$
	Bomb size:	18 kt	0.91 Mt	9.1 Mt
First minute (60 s)		4.2	105	1.05
First hour (3600 s)		8.8	220	2.20
First day (86.4 ks)		10.9	272	2.72
First week (605 ks)		11.6	291	2.91
First month (2.63 Ms)		12.1	301	3.01
First year (31.6 Ms)		12.4	310	3.10
Total (infinity dose)		**12.6**	**314**	**3.14**

Notes:

(a) For an explanation of bomb size designations, see note 2.

(b) The data are derived from those of Glasstone (1964: 424).

(c) The 18 kt bomb is a fission bomb whereas the 0.91 Mt and 9.1 Mt bombs are half fission and half fusion.

(d) The first minute of nuclear radiation is usually referred to as the initial radiation, and what comes after that as the residual radiation. The first day of nuclear radiation is usually referred to as the early radiation.

10

the fall-out of surface materials made radioactive by neutron bombardment and injected into the atmosphere by the blast.

The sources, forms and amounts of nuclear radiation can differ remarkably depending upon bomb type (for example, fission versus fission/fusion; 'clean' versus 'dirty'), bomb size and where detonated (for example, air versus surface versus sub-surface) (Glasstone, 1964: VIII–IX).

The discussion here is based largely upon the biological impact of gamma radiation and, moreover, of gamma radiation whose source is external to the affected organisms. The estimates of impact must therefore be recognized as being somewhat conservative. Within the past several years, the significance of the less penetrating beta radiation (electrons) has come to be understood as an additional insult to the environment (Kantz, 1971; Murphy and McCormick, 1971; Rhoads and Platt, 1971; Rhoads et al., 1971), and inclusion of the beta radiation might increase total dose levels by as much as a factor or two. Moreover, particularly with wildlife, an additional source of radioactive exposure comes from ingested radionuclides such as ^{89}Sr, ^{90}Sr, ^{131}I, ^{137}Cs and perhaps ^{239}Pu. Although such internal exposures would, depending upon feeding habits and other factors, add only 1 per cent to 10 per cent to total exposure, their biological effect can be magnified if the radioactive substance concentrates at a particular location within the body. Strontium and plutonium, for example, tend to concentrate near the bone marrow, iodine in the thyroid gland and caesium in the blood.

The lethal dose levels from nuclear radiation have been summarized for many plants (Sparrow et al., 1971; Sparrow and Sparrow, 1965), for some mammals (Spalding and Holland, 1971) and for various other organisms (Wurtz, 1963). The lethal level for most of the mammals tested (that is, the dose that kills 50 per cent of exposed organisms, or LD_{50}) falls between 0.3 kR and 0.8 kR; the level for man seems to fall between 0.4 kR and 0.5 kR. Birds are killed by dose levels comparable to those that kill mammals. For amphibians and reptiles, the lethal dose appears to be about three times that for mammals.

The lethal dose levels for the higher plants spans the mammalian and reptilian ranges. Many conifers are at the sensitive end of this spectrum and some of the grasses are at the resistant end. All of the higher plants are more resistant to radioactive damage during their dormant periods. Insects for the most part are about a hundred times as resistant as mammals. However, social insects such as honey bees (*Apis mellifera*: Apidae) (important as pollinators) are destroyed by 5 kR (Auerbach, 1968; Goolsby, 1968). Many bacteria, algae and fungi can withstand doses a thousand times greater than those that kill mammals.

The effect of nuclear radiation on the survival of the higher plants can be predicted fairly well, since their chromosome volume (and thus also their degree of polyploidy) turns out to be well correlated with their radio-resistance (Sparrow et al., 1971; Sparrow and Sparrow, 1965). Although this relationship may also hold for insects, it does not appear to hold for mammals (Comroy et al., 1971). Those plants better able to cope with nature's more routine adversities, such as low temperature, drought or wind, are often the more radio-resistant ones (Woodwell, 1967). For both flora and fauna, age and season can influence radio-sensitivity. Moreover, root systems, soil micro-organisms and burrowing animals receive partial shielding by the earth, thereby avoiding some nuclear (as well as thermal) radiation damage (Blumenfeld, 1966).

Table 1.9. Initial nuclear radiation from a nuclear bomb exploded in the troposphere

Nuclear radiation during first 60 s		Size of area receiving more than the given radiation		
	Bomb size:	18 kt	0.91 Mt	9.1 Mt
0.5 kR				
Diameter (km)		2.6	4.4	5.5
Area (ha)		545	1 510	2 380
2 kR				
Diameter (km)		2.0	3.7	4.8
Area (ha)		318	1 080	1 840
10 kR				
Diameter (km)		1.3	2.9	4.0
Area (ha)		129	648	1 250
20 kR				
Diameter (km)		1.0	2.6	3.7
Area (ha)		79	523	1 060
70 kR				
Diameter (km)		0.5	2.0	3.1
Area (ha)		18	312	759

Notes:

(a) For an explanation of bomb size designations, see note 2.

(b) The data are derived from those of Glasstone (1964: 380).

(c) The 18 kt bomb is a fission bomb whereas the 0.91 Mt and 9.1 Mt bombs are half fission and half fusion.

(d) The initial (first 60 s) nuclear radiation provided in the table represents about 33 per cent of the ultimate total (table 1.8).

(e) The explosions are so-called typical air bursts.[5] Comparable data for surface bursts would have diameters roughly 67 per cent and areas 44 per cent of those presented (Glasstone, 1964: 379).

(f) The data presented in this table can also be used as a rough approximation of the contamination patterns for the ultimate total nuclear radiation of an air burst inasmuch as the residual radiation would be dispersed over a vast area (Glasstone, 1964: 415).

12

The impact of massive nuclear radiation on entire ecosystems has been considered in terms of the damage sustained by the dominant vegetation. The dominant vegetation accounts not only for a substantial fraction of the ecosystem's primary production, but also provides shelter for many of the animals in the system. To destroy a coniferous forest (that is, to kill essentially 100 per cent of the dominant vegetation) requires a total dose of about 2 kR; to destroy a temperate dicotyledonous forest requires 10 kR; to destroy grassland (prairie) requires 20 kR; and to destroy a biotype dominated by herbaceous non-grasses (forbs) requires about 70 kR (note 7).

In order to be able to relate all of the above information on lethal levels of nuclear radiation to the ecological impact of a bomb, it is, of

Table 1.10. Early nuclear radiation from a nuclear bomb exploded at the surface

Nuclear radiation during first 24 h		Size of area receiving more than the given radiation		
	Bomb size:	18 kt	0.91 Mt	9.1 Mt
0.5 kR				
Elliptical axes (km)		2.3 × 15.8	14.5 × 83	27.3 × 189
Area (ha)		2 850	94 500	405 000
2 kR				
Elliptical axes (km)		1.1 × 7.8	10.3 × 45	18.8 × 120
Area (ha)		674	36 400	177 000
10 kR				
Elliptical axes (km)		0.7 × 2.7	7.1 × 23	12.7 × 64
Area (ha)		148	12 800	63 800
20 kR				
Elliptical axes (km)		0.6 × 1.6	5.8 × 16	10.6 × 47
Area (ha)		75	7 290	39 100
70 kR				
Elliptical axes (km)		0.5 × 1.1	4.0 × 9	7.0 × 22
Area (ha)		43	2 830	12 100

Notes:

(a) For an explanation of bomb size designations, see note 2.

(b) The data are derived from those of Glasstone (1964: 457, 450, 429).

(c) The 18 kt bomb is a fission bomb, whereas the 0.91 Mt and 9.1 Mt bombs are half fission and half fusion.

(d) The early (first 24 h) nuclear radiation provided in the table represents about 87 per cent of the ultimate total (table 1.8). A uniform wind direction and speed throughout the lower atmosphere of 6.7 m/s as well as no rain are postulated for the entire 24 h period.

(e) Comparable data for a so-called typical air burst[5] would be roughly equivalent to those presented in table 1.9 inasmuch as those presented in the present table are based for the most part on radioactive fallout particles produced from surface materials incorporated into the fireball at the time of detonation.

course, necessary to know how large an area is subjected to such levels. Thus, a 0.91 Mt bomb would destroy coniferous forests over an area of about 1 100 ha if an air burst (Table 1.9), but over perhaps 36×10^3 ha if a surface burst (Table 1.10). Such a bomb would destroy boreal or temperate forest of any sort on about 650 ha if an air burst, or on about 13×10^3 ha if a surface burst. Similarly, grasslands would be destroyed on about 520 ha if an air burst, or on about 7 300 ha if a surface burst.

The same 0.91 Mt bomb would kill most mammals over an area of about 1 500 ha if an air burst, or on about 94×10^3 ha if a surface burst. Such a bomb would destroy most vertebrates on about 1 100 ha if an air burst, or on 36×10^3 ha if a surface burst.

These areas of radioactive contamination for surface bursts (Table 1.10) may be compared with some information released by the USA on one of its large Pacific test explosions. This is the notorious 'Bravo' shot of 1 March 1954 at Bikini (Glasstone, 1964: 460–464; Conard *et al.*, 1975; Lapp, 1958). Considering the differences in yield and so forth, the data do, in fact, coincide rather well (Table 1.11). It is fortunate that the immense zone of lethality created by this trial was able to spend itself over a trackless ocean expanse, at least for the most part.

Table 1.11. Nuclear radiation from the nuclear bomb exploded at the surface at Namu Island, Bikini Atoll, 1 March 1954

Nuclear radiation during first 96 h	Size of area receiving more than the given radiation
0.5 kR	
Elliptical axes (km)	62 × 326
Area (ha)	1 590 000
2 kR	
Elliptical axes (km)	30 × 210
Area (ha)	495 000
10 kR	
Elliptical axes (km)	15 × 100
Area (ha)	118 000

Notes:

(*a*) The bomb was one designated as 13.6 Mt; for an explanation of this designation (Glasstone, 1964: 673), see note 2.

(*b*) The data are derived from those of Glasstone (1964: 462).

(*c*) The bomb (code-named 'Bravo') was about half fission and half fusion (US Atomic Energy Commission, priv. comm., 9 Jan. 1974).

(*d*) The 96 h nuclear radiation provided in the table represents about 92 per cent of the ultimate total (table 1.8). There was no rain during this 96 h period. Based on arrival time, the average wind speed during the first 20 h was 7.4 m/s (Glasstone, 1964: 462).

The discussion in the present section has largely dwelt upon nuclear radiation in terms of lethal levels. There are a number of more subtle long-term effects that can be expected to occur in those organisms exposed to a sublethal dose. These include reduced fertility, shortened life span, higher incidence of neoplasms and increased mutational frequency. Such effects, of deep concern with respect to human populations, seem to have only modest direct significance with respect to the plant and animal populations within an ecosystem. Moreover, following a nuclear detonation, one can expect a slight worldwide increase in the so-called background radiation that will last for years (Kulp, 1965; Nier *et al.*, 1975). The stress imposed by this increase is apparently equivalent to the stresses from other pollutants (Woodwell, 1970) and thus, although almost insignificant by itself, adds to the others.

III. Ecological consequences

General

Once the dust has settled, so to speak, a terrestrial nuclear attack will have left a region devastated by the several intense forms of energy dissipation described in the previous sections. The present section is devoted to the ecological ramifications of such devastation.[8]

In what follows, the environmental impact of nuclear attack is described in three categories: the earth itself or geosphere; the atmosphere overlying this geosphere; and the living things, or biosphere, that live upon and within the geosphere and atmosphere. But first it is necessary to indicate the geographical extent of the devastation being dealt with. The various forms of destruction previously described occur in concert, overlapping and reinforcing each other. A nuclear detonation will desolate several hundred hectares and will have a variety of serious effects that diminish outward over an area of several thousand hectares (Tables 1.12 and 1.13). The area of mortality to living things from nuclear radiation is an extensive one for either air or surface bursts, but is particularly impressive for the latter case. Thus, the nuclear radiation from a 0.91 Mt surface burst will kill most trees over an area of 13×10^3 ha and most vertebrates on 36×10^3 ha (Table 1.13). Another major environmental threat from a nuclear detonation, especially in the less wet regions and seasons, results from the thermal radiation. Under appropriate weather and site conditions, a 0.91 Mt air burst will initiate

Table 1.12. Damage to biota from a nuclear bomb exploded in the troposphere

Type of damage		Area suffering the given type of damage (ha)		
	Bomb size:	18 kt	0.91 Mt	9.1 Mt
Craterization by the blast wave		0	0	0
Trees blown down by the blast wave		565	14 100	82 000
Trees killed by nuclear radiation		129	648	1 250
All vegetation killed by nuclear radiation		18	312	759
Dry vegetation ignited by thermal radiation		1 170	33 300	183 000
Vertebrates killed by the blast wave		43	591	2 740
Vertebrates killed by nuclear radiation		318	1 080	1 840
Vertebrates killed by thermal radiation		1 570	42 000	235 000

Notes:

(a) For an explanation of bomb size designations, see note 2.

(b) Craterization by the blast wave is from Table 1.4. Trees blown down by the blast wave are from Table 1.2, using the 90 per cent blowdown data. Tree mortality by nuclear radiation is from Table 1.9, using the 10 kR data. All-vegetation mortality by nuclear radiation is from Table 1.9, using the 70 kR data. Dry vegetation ignitions by thermal radiation is from Table 1.7, using the 500 kJ/m^2 datum for the 18 kt bomb, the 750 kJ/m^2 datum for the 0.91 Mt bomb, and the 1 000 kJ/m^2 datum for the 9.1 Mt bomb (cf. Table 1.5). Vertebrate mortality by the blast wave is from Table 1.3, using the lethal-to-50 per cent data. Vertebrate mortality by nuclear radiation is from Table 1.9, using the 2 kR data. Vertebrate mortality by thermal radiation is from Table 1.6, using the lethal-to-50 per cent data for interpolation in Table 1.7.

(c) The 18 kt bomb is a fission bomb, whereas the 0.91 Mt and 9.1 Mt bombs are half fission and half fusion.

(d) The explosions are so-called typical air bursts.[5] Comparable data for surface bursts are presented in Table 1.13.

wildfires over perhaps 33×10^3 ha and burn to death most vertebrates on 42×10^3 (Table 1.12). Hypothetical scenarios of a nuclear attack against the conterminous United States, with its 783×10^6 ha of land, often suggest a total expenditure of between 5×10^3 Mt and 10×10^3 Mt, divided half and half between air and surface bursts and with the shots centred upon urban, industrial and military targets.

Geosphere

A matter of major concern is the site degradation that will occur over

Table 1.13. Damage to biota from a nuclear bomb exploded at the surface

Type of damage		Area suffering the given type of damage (ha)		
	Bomb size:	18 kt	0.91 Mt	9.1 Mt
Craterization by the blast wave		1	12	57
Trees blown down by the blast wave		362	9 040	52 500
Trees killed by nuclear radiation		148	12 800	63 800
All vegetation killed by nuclear radiation		43	2 830	12 100
Dry vegetation ignited by thermal radiation		749	21 300	117 000
Vertebrates killed by the blast wave		24	332	1 540
Vertebrates killed by nuclear radiation		674	36 400	177 000
Vertebrates killed by thermal radiation		1 000	26 900	150 000

Notes:

(a) For an explanation of bomb size designations, see note 2.

(b) Craterization by the blast wave is from Table 1.4. Trees blown down by the blast wave is from Table 1.2, using the 90 per cent blowdown data reduced to 64 per cent of the given values to convert to surface burst. Tree mortality by nuclear radiation is from Table 1.10, using the 10 kR data. All-vegetation mortality by nuclear radiation is from Table 1.10, using the 70 kR data. Dry vegetation ignitions by thermal radiation is from Table 1.7, using the 500 kJ/m^2 datum for the 18 kt bomb, the 750 kJ/m^2 datum for the 0.91 Mt bomb, and the 1 000 kJ/m^2 datum for the 9.1 Mt bomb (cf. Table 1.5), all reduced to 64 per cent of the given values to convert to surface burst. Vertebrate mortality by the blast wave is from Table 1.3, using the lethal-to-50 per cent data reduced to 56 per cent of the given values to convert to surface burst. Vertebrate mortality by nuclear radiation is from Table 1.10, using the 2 kR data. Vertebrate mortality by thermal radiation is from Table 1.6, using the lethal-to-50 per cent data for interpolation in Table 1.7, then reduced to 64 per cent of the values obtained to convert to surface burst.

(c) The 18 kt bomb is a fission bomb, whereas the 0.91 Mt and 9.1 Mt bombs are half fission and half fusion.

(d) Comparable data for so-called typical air bursts[5] are presented in Table 1.12.

the entire area of a nuclear attack as a result of greatly accelerated wind and water erosion (Craft, 1964; Katz, 1966). A related concern is the accelerated loss to the area of minerals in solution, that is, of nutrient dumping. These insults to the geomass of an ecosystem will be especially pronounced while the region in question remains barren or sparsely vegetated. Moreover, the fires associated with the nuclear attack would aggravate these situations. Severe and extensive site degradation of these sorts could extend the time required for ecological recovery by many years or decades beyond what might be expected on the basis of past experience.

The damage to the geosphere just alluded to refers to its terrestrial fraction, sometimes called the lithosphere. The aquatic fraction, or hydrosphere, would also be subjected to some abuse. Unless it is a direct target (Glasstone, 1964: VI), the damage is, however, at a more modest level and is not further discussed here (see Nier et al., 1975: 102–161).

Atmosphere

The question arises as to how a nuclear attack will alter the atmospheric conditions and thereby the weather.[9] It appears that the two most likely sources of ecological disturbance of the atmosphere would arise from the injection into the stratosphere[4] of dust particles (particulate aerosol) on the one hand, and of oxides of nitrogen (for example, NO, NO_2) on the other.

Surface bursts blast out huge craters. Some of the displaced material – perhaps 0.5 per cent of it (Nier et al., 1975: 54) – is injected into the stratosphere as a fine dust. For a 0.91 Mt bomb, this would thus amount to perhaps $19 \times 10^3 \text{ m}^3$ (50×10^6 kg) of material (Table 1.4). The stratospheric residence time of this dust would be up to several years. Such aerosol supplies condensation nuclei for cloud formation. It also acts as a partial barrier to radiation to and from the earth, both in its own right and as a result of the clouds formed.

One of the major volcanic eruptions within the past century occurred at Krakatoa Island, Indonesia (latitude 6° S), in August 1883. This event has been calculated to have introduced a dust veil into the stratosphere consisting of about $30 \times 10^6 \text{ m}^3$ (80×10^9 kg) of fine tephra.[10] This stratospheric particulate aerosol contamination is claimed to have resulted in the lowering of temperatures in the mid latitudes of the southern hemisphere by possibly as much as 0.5°C, and in the mid latitudes of the northern by possibly as much as 0.2°C, these depressions diminishing to zero during a period of about 38 months (Lamb, 1970: 475, 519; Budyko, 1971: 444; see also Pollack et al., 1976). A modest change in temperature can, of course, have some ecological ramifications.[11] The dust veil also had other modest atmospheric effects on a global scale that persisted for at least five years after the event (Ingersoll, 1963: II; 1964–1965; Meinel and Meinel, 1967).

About 1 600 0·91 Mt nuclear bombs detonated as surface bursts would introduce approximately as much fine particulate matter into the stratosphere as did Krakatoa. (Sub-surface bursts could reduce this number to about 130 (Table 1.4: note e).)

Aerial bursts generate immense amounts of several odd oxides of nitrogen. Some fraction of these chemical species finds its way into the lower stratosphere where it catalytically degrades the ozone (O_3) to ordinary oxygen gas (O_2). Such a depletion of the ozone layer permits, among other things, a greater fraction of the solar ultra-violet radiation to reach the earth, especially that biologically active portion in the wavelength range of approximately 280 nm to 315 nm (so-called UV-B) (Cutchis, 1974; Johnson, 1973).

It has been suggested that to destroy 50 per cent of the ozone layer of either the northern or the southern hemisphere would require the detonation of some 10^4 0.91 Mt bombs in the troposphere of that hemisphere, with recovery progressing at about 8 per cent per year (Bauer and Gilmore, 1975; Johnston et al., 1973; Nier et al., 1975: 42; Whitten and Borucki, 1975). If the bombs were detonated in the upper atmosphere, then a considerably lower number might be required to achieve the same level of effect (Hampson, 1974). A 50 per cent depletion in the ozone layer would increase the amount of ultra-violet radiation reaching the ground by a factor of three or more (Cutchis, 1974; Reid et al., 1976: 179). Under normal circumstances in the mid latitudes (and at any elevation below about 2 000 m), a similar increase in ultra-violet radiation would be achieved by shifting toward the equator by about 16° of latitude (ca. 1 800 km) (Cutchis, 1974). As to distance above sea level, there is virtually no effect on ultra-violet exposure in the biologically active range between 280 nm and 315 nm up to 1 500 m or so; above that elevation, exposure can be taken to increase by roughly 1 per cent per 100 m for at least the next 3 000 m (Caldwell, 1968).

Ultra-violet radiation (especially at wavelengths shorter than about 300 nm) has the ability to damage various macro-molecules such as deoxyribonucleic acid (DNA) and proteins, and thereby the cells and thus the organisms of which they are a part (Giese, 1964–1973; Urbach, 1969). Small organisms, especially micro-organisms are, by virtue of their surface-to-volume ratio, *potentially* more vulnerable to such damage than large ones. Moreover, fauna active in the open and during daytime are, by virtue of these habits, *potentially* more vulnerable than secretive and nocturnal ones. On the other hand, the small and the more exposed organisms for various other reasons are likely to be less prone to ultra-violet damage.

The ecological significance of ultra-violet enrichment of the environment has been considered, at least superficially, by a number of authors (Eigner, 1975; Hampson, 1974; Johnston, 1974 a, b; Nier et al., 1975; Reid et al., 1976; Ruderman, 1974). The impact would, of course, depend upon the level and duration of enrichment. On the basis of the largely hypothetical information currently available, it seems that tropospheric bursts totalling the 9×10^3 Mt discussed above would exert only a marginal influence on natural ecosystems via the transient ultra-violet enrichment of the environment that would result. This supposition finds some support in the researches of Caldwell (1968) with plants growing in the field under a modest diversity of ultra-violet regimes; and also in the reviews by Caldwell (1971) and Levitt (1972: 453–459). The possible impact of ambient ultra-violet enhancement on humans is noted below.

Biosphere

Ecological recovery of both the barren and partially destroyed areas resulting from a nuclear attack can be expected to soon begin. Indeed, some pertinent observations on such recolonization and subsequent succession are available from actual nuclear test sites. One of these is situated in the Mohave (Great Basin) Desert in Nevada (Allred *et al.*, 1965; Schultz, 1966). In addition to more than a dozen underground tests, this site was subjected over an eight-year period to at least 89 small above-ground detonations (the majority of them air bursts[5] averaging 10.1 kg each, and with the largest being 67.1 kg (Glasstone, 1964: 439, 671 ff). One is indebted to Shields and her colleagues for the following information (Rickard and Shields, 1963; Shields and Rickard, 1961; Shields and Wells, 1962; 1963; Shields *et al.*, 1963).

Initially each of the detonations had totally cleaned an area of all life, an area that ranged in size between 73 ha and 204 ha. Depending upon local site conditions (and presumably also on type of device, yield and type of burst), the original zone of complete or severe vegetational damage per detonation was roughly 400 ha to 1 375 ha in size. No evidence was detected of initial vegetational damage at any explosion site beyond an area of approximately 3 255 ha. The denuded central areas were invaded by pioneer species over a period of three to four years and the adjacent zones of severe damage also began their slow process of ecological recovery. So far as could be recognized, the subsequent pattern of succession was of the sort and rate to be expected in this desert region following any severe disturbance of the habitat, a process spanning many decades.

Biologists have also studied nuclear test sites in the tropical Pacific area (Berrill, 1966; Hines, 1962). As reported by Palumbo (1962) and Held (1960) for Eniwetok Island and by Fosberg (1959 a, b) for several islands in Rongelap Atoll and elsewhere, vegetational recovery from nuclear devastation seems to take its normal, here relatively rapid, successional course. In a study of the effect of radionuclides with particular reference to the omnivorous land crab *Coenobita perlatus* (Coenobitidae), Held (1960) noted that the population of this crab soon returned to normal following the nuclear testing on Eniwetok. Two years after testing, moreover, ^{90}Sr, ^{137}Cs and ^{144}Ce seemed to have established themselves permanently in the biogeochemical cycling involving *Coenobita*. Also on Eniwetok, Jackson (1969) was able to attribute the local extinction of the Polynesian rat (*Rattus exulans*; Muridae) to the nuclear testing there.

It seems from the above evidence that biotic recovery can be expected to more or less follow the normal patterns of ecological succession for the region in question. Unfortunately, the above picture may not be the whole story. For one thing, vegetational recovery will be hindered to the extent that seed sources are no longer available in a region, a function of the severity and geographical extent of the attack. Another serious concern is the question of ecosystem stability. The numerous plants and animals in a region differ widely in their relative radio-sensitivities as well as to the other insults of a nuclear attack. As a result, many subtle and some not so subtle imbalances could be created in the predator/prey, host/parasite, and endless other species interactions that form the very basis of an ecosystem. In particular, troubles might arise as a result of the relative radio-resistances exhibited by certain taxa such as the insects, bacteria and fungi – all of which are capable of causing mischief, both to man and nature.

It is rather difficult to prognosticate on the particulars of ecosystem stability following an attack, or rather on the lack of it. First of all, one is dealing with a system of pioneer communities, with their limited species diversity and notorious instability. Secondly, the considerations of relative radio- and other sensitivities mentioned earlier will be complicated by the different relative reproductive potentials of the species. Thirdly, animals have different feeding habits, and lie at different positions in the food web. The tendency for some radionuclides to become more concentrated as they work their way up this ladder will provide a disproportionate stress on the carnivores (including man) at the top. Thus, to generalize, one might expect the populations of the more specialized animals (specialized with respect to either their food or physical site requirements) to be most seriously affected initially and to recover their former status most slowly through the years.

The simplified, early-successional ecosystems that can be expected to establish themselves in a region subjected to nuclear attack will not only be relatively unstable for the reasons suggested, but will also be inferior because of their considerably reduced biomass. The biomass will be even lower than that predicted on the basis of experience with ecological recovery from disruption by non-nuclear means. Trees are in general more radio-sensitive than shrubs, high shrubs more than low shrubs, woody plants more than herbaceous plants, and angiosperms more than mosses and lichens (Sparrow *et al.*, 1971; Sparrow and Sparrow, 1965; Whicker and Fraley, 1974; Woodwell, 1967; Woodwell and Holt, 1971). A reduced biomass results in reduced ecosystem productivity, reduced, for example, by as much as 80 per cent in a change from forest to grassland.

Finally, it has been suggested that a nuclear attack involving about 9×10^3 Mt might depress global temperatures by several tenths of a degree Celsius, with recovery occurring over a period of several years (Nier *et al.*, 1975). There might thus also be some modest concomitant alteration in the amount of precipitation. This suggestion seems to be an exaggeration although, if true, a change in the weather of this magnitude could depress agricultural productivity, at least for some crops, by perhaps 1 per cent (note 12).

IV. Conclusion

Uncertainty may exist about the future likelihood of nuclear war. On the other hand, there is no doubt that nuclear weapons should be eliminated from the military arsenals of the world. Even the most modest and restrained nuclear initiative by one belligerent could well be countered in kind, this in turn perhaps leading to an escalating exchange. The USA and the USSR are said each to possess sufficient nuclear might to destroy not only each other, but all human life on earth. England, France, China, India and perhaps other nations possess more modest nuclear arsenals. Despite desultory negotiations in the face of the already existing overkill, the arms race between the USA and the USSR continues for ever more and better bombs, ever more and better delivery systems and ever more though largely illusory countermeasures (SIPRI, 1975 d; Scoville and Osborn, 1970; Epstein, 1976; SIPRI, 1974 b; York, 1970).

Even the very limited nuclear attacks by the United States during World War II had a profound impact on man, his artifacts and his social systems. The immediate social consequences of such attack, largely beyond the scope of this book, have been well captured by a number of eyewitnesses and other authors.[13] A word is in order, however, on the long-term effects on human health.

The subtle effects of nuclear war are of long duration, as the very thorough, continuing studies of the survivors of Hiroshima and Nagasaki have demonstrated (Miller, 1974; Blot and Miller, 1973; Wood et al., 1967; Lifton, 1967; Okada et al., 1975). The more important disorders that have been noted among those survivors include increased incidence of leukaemia, thyroid tumours, lenticular opacities and chromosomal aberrations in the peripheral blood lymphocytes. For the survivors who were infants at the time of the blasts, this list must be extended to include modest impairment in growth and development. For the survivors who were *in utero* at the time, it must be extended once again, this time to include microcephaly and mental retardation.

The Hiroshima and Nagasaki findings have found independent confirmation from the also very detailed and long-term studies of the survivors of the test detonation of the 13.6 Mt fission/fusion device of 1 March 1954 at Bikini that was described earlier. This event continues to take its human toll among the accidentally exposed group (Conard et al., 1975). More than 100 persons unfortunately were within about 185 km of the detonation (23 on a fishing vessel and 89 on Rongelap Atoll) and were as a result exposed to roughly 0.2 kR of nuclear radiation from the early fall-out. Several deaths as well as a substantial number of tumours, some of them malignant, are attributable to this exposure. Included is an especially high frequency of thyroid tumours among those who were children or *in utero* at the time – and the number of these cases continues to rise.

US testing ended at Bikini and Eniwetok in 1958. In August 1975 the US Energy Research and Development Administration (successor to the US Atomic Energy Commission) found Bikini not yet habitable owing to the continued radioactive contamination of the drinking water and vegetation (Nordheimer, 1975). Two decades has, however, sufficed for Eniwetok (now Enewetak) to attain a presumably safe level (Wilford, 1977).

There has been some recent speculation on the effects on human health that a major nuclear exchange might have via atmospheric alterations of a widespread nature (Ahmed, 1975). One concern involves the increase in skin cancers that would result from ultra-violet enrichment of the environment owing to depletion of the stratospheric ozone layer. On the assumption that the geographical differences in non-melanoma skin cancer frequency reported by Scotto et al. (1974) are attributable to the normal latitudinal differences in ultra-violet intensity and on the basis of the correlation reported by Cutchis (1974) between the amount of stratospheric ozone and the intensity of ultra-violet radiation reaching the earth, Nier et al. (1975: 185–200) calculated that nuclear bursts in the troposphere of the northern hemisphere totalling 9×10^3 Mt would (assuming no avoidance behaviour) increase the normal frequency of skin cancers in that hemisphere by about 10 per cent, a value that would diminish to zero over the subsequent nine decades.[14]

The nuclear arms race is a danger even without war. Not only are natural resources squandered in the production of a nuclear arsenal, but the earth is subsequently polluted with worrisome amounts of radioactive isotopes during the manufacture and especially the testing of the weapons. Moreover, McPhee (1973) and Willrich and Taylor (1974), among others, have recently publicized the potential threat of nuclear weapons falling into the hands of irresponsible subnational groups or even individuals.

In closing, it must be reiterated that a major nuclear exchange must be avoided at all costs for it would have prohibitive consequences for both man and nature.

Notes to Chapter 1

1. There is a voluminous literature dealing with nuclear weapons and nuclear war. It runs the gamut from descriptive to theoretical, from scientific to polemical, from simple to complex and from accessible to unavailable. Glasstone (1964) provides the single most useful source for the technical aspects of nuclear weapons and their effects (another revision is in progress). See also the report by the Defense Civil Preparedness Agency (1973). For an excellent over-all summary of the effects of nuclear weapons and on the implications of their employment, see Vellodi et al. (1968). Other brief summaries are also available (ACDA, n.d., 1975?; Health, Education and Welfare, 1959 c; Brode, 1968). See also the bibliography by O'Callaghan (1973).

   Descriptions of the ecological impact of nuclear weapons and war are cited in note 8 and of the social impact in note 13.

2. Nuclear bombs are categorized according to their size, that is, energy yield, in terms of the yield of an equivalent weight of 2,4,6-trinitrotoluene (TNT). The energy yield (or 'heat of explosion') of TNT by definition is taken to be 4.615×10^6 J/kg (Kinney, 1962: 2). The kilotonne (kt) used here as a measure of nuclear bomb size thus designates an energy yield from 10^6 kg of 'defined' TNT or 4.615×10^{12} J; similarly, one megatonne (Mt) is in this context the equivalent of 10^9 kg of TNT releasing 4.615×10^{15} J. The S.I. prefixes 'k-' and 'M-' are employed here with 'tonne' in the context of nuclear weapons despite the inappropriateness of this procedure, owing to common usage.

   Unfortunately, the term 'kiloton' as used by the US Department of Defense and other US agencies is the equivalent of 0.907×10^6 kg of TNT (4.187×10^{12} J) and its 'megaton' of 0.907×10^9 kg of TNT (4.187×10^{15} J).

   Two basic categories of nuclear bombs exist: (1) the atomic bomb, which relies on the complete fission of about 64.8 g/kt of ^{235}U and/or ^{239}Pu; and (2) the hydrogen bomb, which relies on fission to trigger the fusion of H isotopes (for purposes of approximation, the yield of this latter bomb being considered to be half from fission and half from fusion). A bomb relying on the fission of ^{235}U is about 5 per cent efficient and thus contains about 1.30 kg/kt of fission yield whereas one relying on ^{239}Pu is about 15 per cent efficient and thus contains about 432 g/kt of fission yield (Vellodi et al., 1968: 54–55). The atomic bombs are usually in the kilotonne range, whereas the hydrogen bombs are usually in the megatonne but can also be in the kilotonne range. About 50 per cent of the energy yield of atomic bombs is released in the form of a blast (shock) wave, about 35 per cent as thermal radiation and the remaining 15 per cent as nuclear radiation (Table 1.1). The comparable values for hydrogen bombs are about 54.5 per cent, 38 per cent and 7.5 per cent, respectively.

The fission reaction of a nuclear bomb produces about 320×10^{21} fission fragments per kilotonne of fission yield (UNSCEAR, 1972: 57) weighing about 62.5 g (Glasstone, 1964: 417), these two values, it is assumed, referring to the situation 1 h after the detonation. On the basis of Avogadro's number (602×10^{21} particles/mol), the fission products per kilotonne of fission bomb after 1 h thus represent the equivalent of 531 mmol of a conglomerate of radioactive isotopes having an average mass number of 118. This mixture (the result of both fission and neutron activation) contains some 200 isotopes of about three dozen elements.

The fusion reaction of a hydrogen bomb results in an excess of between 10^{23} and 10^{24} atoms of ^3H per kilotonne of fusion yield (UNSCEAR, 1972: 57). Using the geometric mean of these two extremes, that is, 316×10^{21} and dividing this value by Avogadro's number as well as by the mass number (that is, 3), one arrives at 175 mg of ^3H per kilotonne of fusion yield.

To recapitulate, a 1 kt atomic (fission) bomb produces about 62.5 g of mixed fission products (that is, as determined 1 h after detonation). A 1 Mt hydrogen bomb ($\frac{1}{2}$ fission, $\frac{1}{2}$ fusion) produces about 31.25 kg of mixed fission products plus about 87.4 g of ^3H.

The numerous fission products of a nuclear bomb decay at greatly different rates. One hour after the detonation of an atomic (fission) bomb there are said to be 440 MCi/kt of fission yield (Shapiro, 1974: 6), that is, 7 055 MCi/kg of mixed fission products. The ^3H disseminated by a fusion reaction (with its half-life of 12.26 years) has a decay rate of 10.12 MCi/kg. Thus, 1 h after the detonation of a hydrogen bomb ($\frac{1}{2}$ fission, $\frac{1}{2}$ fusion) there would be 220 500 MCi/Mt from the mixed fission products plus about 976 kCi/Mt from the ^3H.

Most of the fission products are extremely short-lived. Their combined decay rate during the initial half year approximates a log/log linear curve having a slope of -1.2; thereafter the over-all decay rate becomes even more rapid, following a new log/log linear curve of slope -2.3 (Glasstone, 1964: 420). In other words, 50 per cent of the fission products present at 1 h after detonation have disappeared about 1.78 h after detonation, 90 per cent about 6.81 h after detonation, 99 per cent about 46.4 h after detonation and 99.9 per cent about 316 h (13.2 d) after detonation. About 42.6 parts per million (ppm) remain after half a year and about 8.66 ppm after one year. One hundred days after detonation is sometimes used as a reference point. If what remains at 100 d (that is, 87.85 ppm of the 1 h value) is taken as 100 per cent, then 48.5 per cent remains half a year after detonation and 9.86 per cent remains one year after detonation.

These decay parameters can also be expressed more directly in relation to the nuclear bombs themselves. For a fission bomb, the 440 MCi/kt that obtains at 1 h has decayed to 38.7 kCi/kt after 100 d and to 3.81 kCi/kt after one year. (Thus, at 100 d there are 620 kCi/kg of original fission products.) For a hydrogen bomb, the 220 500

MCi/Mt of mixed fission products obtaining at 1 h have decayed to 19.4 MCi/Mt after 100 d and to 1.91 MCi/Mt after one year. The latter bomb's 976 kCi/Mt of ^{3}H present at 1 h decays to 960 kCi/Mt after 100 d and to 922 kCi/Mt after one year. On the other hand, a small but biologically important group of fission products is rather long-lived (that is, with half-lives measurable in years), including ^{90}Sr and ^{137}Cs.

Three bomb sizes are often used in the present text for purposes of illustration: 18 kt (88.736 × 10^{12} J), 0.91 Mt (4.187 × 10^{15} J) and 9.1 Mt (41.868 × 10^{15} J). These are equivalent to 20 'kilotons', 1 'megaton' and 10 'megatons', respectively, in common US terminology. The 18 kt bomb used is a fission bomb whereas the 0.91 Mt and 9.1 Mt bombs are half fission and half fusion. When air bursts are given, these refer to so-called typical air bursts[5].

3. Of the 14.3 × 10^9 kg of conventional munitions expended by the USA during the Second Indochina War, it can be estimated that 74 per cent contained high explosives; for this fraction an explosive content of 35 per cent is estimated. One can thus calculate an explosive energy yield[2] for that war of approximately 3.7 Mt. Expenditures by the other side would add an insignificant amount to this value, of the order of 0.01 Mt.

4. The earth's atmosphere extends upward very roughly 150 km. It is divided into the lower atmosphere, which represents more than 99 per cent of the atmospheric mass, and the upper atmosphere with less than 1 per cent of the mass. In the concentric atmospheric spheres given below the paranthetically noted altitudinal bands can only be given as rough approximations since the values vary appreciably with both latitude and season.

The lower atmosphere (ca. 0–55 km) is divided into the troposphere (ca. 0–12 km), which represents more than 87 per cent of the atmospheric mass, and the stratosphere (ca. 12–55 km), about 12 per cent of the mass. The stratosphere, in turn, can be divided into the lower stratosphere (ca. 12–30 km) and the upper stratosphere (ca. 30–55 km).

Some ozone is found throughout the atmosphere, its over-all average concentration being 635 μg/kg (820 μg/m^3). Thus, at 0°C and 101 kPa, i.e., at 'standard' temperature and pressure (STP), the atmospheric ozone would constitute a band with an average thickness of about 3.1 mm. The atmospheric ozone is not distributed evenly, but is found largely in the lower stratosphere, indeed, largely within a so-called ozone layer (ca. 20–30 km) in which the atmospheric concentration of ozone is up to a hundred times the over-all average.

The upper atmosphere (ca. 55–150 km) is divided into the mesosphere (ca. 55–80 km) and the ionosphere (= thermosphere) (ca. 80–150 km).

The charged high-energy particles comprising the Van Allen belt (= magnetosphere) (ca. 250–25 000 km) are well above the atmosphere.

5. The explosion of a nuclear bomb is classed as an air burst when it occurs within the lower atmosphere (see note 4), but at an altitude sufficiently high that its fireball does not touch the earth's surface. For an 18 kt bomb, this minimum altitude is 186 m, for a 0.91 Mt bomb it is 853 m and for a 9.1 Mt bomb it is 2 195 m (Glasstone, 1964: 79).

The optimal height for an air burst – a so-called typical air burst – is within the troposphere,[4] varying with bomb size. A 'typical' air burst of an 18 kt bomb is at an altitude of 564 m, for a 0·91 Mt bomb it is at 2 077 m and for a 9·1 Mt bomb it is at 4 476 m (Glasstone, 1964: 114, 127, 638). Air bursts in the present text are these 'typical' ones.

6. The likelihood, extent and consequences of fires brought about by nuclear attack have been dealt with by Glasstone (1964: VII), Broido (1960; 1963), Chandler et al.

(1963), Craft (1964), Defense Civil Preparedness Agency (1973: III), Hill (1961), Huschke (1966), Ayres (1965: Vol. I:II) and others. See also Chapter 3.

7. The data presented have been estimated by Woodwell and Sparrow (1963). Seemingly comparable measurements by Platt (1963) for similar ecosystems have yielded values up to twice as high. However, the data used here have more recently been confirmed by Woodwell and Holt (1971). They also find support in related data provided by Sparrow *et al.* (1971). The coniferous forest value is supported by OKunewick (1966). Whicker and Fraley (1974) agree with the coniferous and temperate dicotyledonous values presented, but suggest that the grassland value should be 100 kR. They add that to destroy tropical rain forest would require 40 kR; and to destroy a moss–lichen community would require 500 kR.

8. The ecological impact of nuclear weapons or war has been reviewed by Ayres (1965), Eberhardt (1967), Glass (1962), Hollister and Eberhardt (1965), Mitchell (1961), Nier *et al.* (1975), Osburn (1968), Platt (1963), Stonier (1964: XI–XII), Wolfe (1959), Woodwell (1963), Woodwell and Holt (1971), Woodwell and Sparrow (1963), Wurtz (1963) and others (see also Parker and Healy, 1955; Whicker and Fraley, 1974).

    For the relationship of nuclear weapons or war to fire, see note 6; for the relationship to weather, see note 9.

9. The impact of nuclear weapons on the weather has been discussed by Ayres (1965: Vol. I: III), Batten (1966), Mason (1955), Nier *et al.* (1975: 24–63), Stonier (1964: XII) and others. See also the bibliography by O'Callaghan (1973). The manipulation of rainfall for hostile purposes is described in Chapter 3.

10. The amount of fine tephra (particulate aerosol ejecta) that in August 1883 was introduced by Krakatoa into the atmosphere or, more to the point here, into the stratosphere[4] is not known with any degree of accuracy. The very few more-or-less independent modern estimates follow. A number of other values have been published in the last several years, but these all seem to be either derivations or misderivations of one or more of those noted here. A density of 2 650 kg/m^3 is assumed (Lutz and Chandler, 1946: 236; Daly *et al.*, 1966).

    To begin with, Lamb (1970: 475, 519; priv. comm., 26 Feb. 1976) estimates that the total amount of fine tephra injected into the *atmosphere* as a whole was about 6×10^9 m (16×10^{12} kg). Mitchell (1970: 146; priv. comm., 27 Feb. 1976) estimates that the amount injected into the *stratosphere* alone was 19×10^6 m^3 (50×10^9 kg). And Deirmendjian (1973: 293; priv. comm., 8 Mar. 1976) estimates the stratospheric injection as having been 30×10^6 m^3 (80×10^9 kg). Deirmendjian's value is adopted here as the most reliable one currently available.

11. Some idea of the ecological impact of *sustained* temperature differentials can be obtained by comparing natural ecosystems along extended north–south transects; or, alternatively, at different altitudes without change in latitude. Air temperature drops more or less uniformly with increasing altitude within the troposphere at a rate that averages 6.4°C/km (Strahler, 1975: 105). By way of comparison, the mean July temperature in the northern hemisphere decreases as one travels northward by roughly 0·58°C per degree of north latitude (or 5.3°C per 1 000 km) (after *Times*, 1968: Plate 5). In order words, a rise in altitude of about 91 m provides a decrease in average summer air temperature comparable to a northward move of 1° of latitude (that is, a rise in altitude of about 820 m is in this respect the equivalent of a northward shift of 1 000 km).

    The following additional data are derived from those of Spurr and Barnes (1973: 96–97) and find support in those of Lutz and Chandler (1946: 267–268). In the eastern USA, a 1°C change in average annual air temperature is achieved by shifting due north or south by 00° 54′ of latitude, that is, by 100 km. The same change can be achieved by shifting up or down by 183 m of elevation. In the western USA, a 1°C change in average annual air temperature is achieved by shifting due north or south by 01° 17′ of latitude, that is, by 143 km. The same change can be achieved by shifting up or down by 157 m of elevation.

For information on the extent to which modest changes in temperature (and of precipitation) influence agricultural productivity, see note 12.

12. The impact of changes in normal weather (precipitation and temperature) on agricultural productivity has been investigated in some detail. For a recent description of the subject, see Thompson (1975), who has been among those in the forefront of this field (Thompson, 1969 a, b; 1970). McQuigg (1975) has prepared a well annotated bibliography on the subject. Three mid-latitude examples will suggest the magnitudes of change to be expected in agricultural productivity as a result of modest and transitory changes in the weather. More drastic effects could be expected locally, especially at the limits of a crop's range or under otherwise marginal conditions.

In the central United States, a 10 mm drop in July rainfall will decrease the yield of corn (*Zea mays;* Gramineae) by about 95 kg/ha (Thompson, 1969 a; see also Runge, 1969–1970). At a yield of 5 375 kg/ha (the US corn belt average for 1967), this represents a decline of 1.8 per cent. A 1°C decrease from the optimal temperature during any month of the growing season will result in essentially no change in yield (unless it occurs during the first month). On the other hand, a similar increase will decrease yield between 100 kg/ha and 200 kg/ha, depending upon the month, that is, by 1.9 to 3.7 per cent.

In the central United States, a 10 mm drop in either July or August rainfall will decrease the yield of soybeans (*Glycine max;* Leguminosae) by about 35 kg/ha (Thompson, 1970). At a yield of 1 800 kg/ha (the approximate central states average for 1967) this represents a decline of 1.9 per cent. A 1°C decrease from the optimal temperature during July will decrease yield by about 45 kg/ha, that is, by 2.5 per cent. A similar increase of 1°C will decrease the yield even more, by about 80 kg/ha, that is, by 4.4 per cent.

The carrying capacity of range lands (grasslands) is also affected by precipitation. The following data are derived from those of Chapline and Cooperrider (1941) for the western United States. From about 200 mm to 600 mm of annual precipitation (normal for grasslands), every additional 44 mm of annual precipitation provides forage for one additional cow (*Bos taurus;* Bovidae) per 100 ha. At an annual precipitation of 400 mm, these range lands can support 6.37 cows/100 ha. A 10 mm decrease in the annual precipitation reduces this value by 0.225 cow/100 ha, that is, by 3.5 per cent.

Modest changes in the weather can also influence the incidence of diseases and insect attack of crops, forest trees, and other plants (Foister, 1935; Graham, 1956: 262–265; Hepting, 1963; Valli, 1966), of livestock and other animals (Smith, 1970), and of humans (Sargent and Tromp, 1964). See also Chapter 3.

For information on how the temperature changes with latitude or altitude, see note 11.

13. The social or human impact of nuclear weapons or war has been reviewed many times. The damage caused by the 13 kt and 21 kt nuclear-fission air bursts over Hiroshima and Nagasaki, respectively has been well captured by Siemes (1946–1947), Hersey (1946), Hachiya (1955), Nagai (1951), Liebow (1965–1966) and D'Olier et al. (1946), among others. Vellodi et al. (1968) have prepared a succinct summary of these World War II data. They also describe the probable impact of a 1 Mt ground burst on a real (though unnamed) city of 1.2×10^6 inhabitants and go on to outline the probable

28

effects of other, more extensive attacks. The postulated short-term consequences of 18 Mt ground or air bursts in the middle of New York City have been vividly described – in brief by the Scientists' Committee for Radiation Information (1962) and at some length by Stonier (1963). Ervin *et al.* (1962) have provided a similar discussion for Boston from a somewhat different perspective. Holifield (1959) gathered much information on what might result from a 3 580 Mt attack on the USA and its overseas bases (with all of the bombs detonated at ground level; each half fission and half fusion). Commoner (1966: V) speculates briefly on the impact of nuclear war. Stonier (1964) provides an extended scenario as a follow-up of his earlier article (Stonier, 1963). York (1975) explains the ease with which Europe would be destroyed by a nuclear exchange between the NATO and Warsaw Pact nations. And a detailed description of what a nuclear attack would do to West Germany has been compiled (Weizsäcker, 1971).

The single most useful source of technical information is by Glasstone (1964). Recovery after an attack has been covered by a number of authors (Wigner *et al.*, 1969; Health, Education and Welfare, 1959 c; Defense Civil Preparedness Agency, 1973) and a number of partially relevant bibliographies exist (Popper and Lybrand, 1960; Rayner, 1957–1958; Quarantelli, 1970).

Post-attack problems of an immediate nature are examined by Aronow *et al.* (1963). The likelihood of plague epidemics following nuclear attack is assessed by Mitchell (1966). Various long-range problems of human health following nuclear war, especially those deriving from nuclear radiation, have been examined numerous times (Edvarson, 1975; Ervin *et al.*, 1962; Glass, 1962; Glasstone, 1964: VIII–XII; Nier *et al.*, 1975: 162–212; Schubert and Lapp, 1957; Arena, 1971; UNSCEAR, 1972; Vellodi *et al.*, 1968; Wood *et al.*, 1967; Miller, 1974; Conard *et al.*, 1975; Okada *et al.*, 1975).

Effects on agriculture and questions of post-attack recovery have been brought together in greatest detail by Bensen and Sparrow (1971). A number of additional sources of such information also exist (Ayres, 1965: Vol. II; Fowler, 1965; Katz, 1966; National Academy of Sciences *et al.*, 1968; Nier *et al.*, 1975: 80–101; Slater *et al.*, 1960; Sparrow *et al.*, 1971).

Finally, attention should be drawn to the very powerful film *The War Game* by Watkins (1966) which depicts the presumed results of a nuclear attack on an industrial city. Moreover, and its shortcomings notwithstanding (Inglis, 1968; Shapiro, 1974), one can further recommend the fictional account by Shute (1957) of what might well be the aftermath of some major nuclear exchange of the future, especially one employing 'dirty' bombs and techniques.

14. Scotto *et al.* (1974) seem to provide the best published data that permit an analysis of the probable relationship between the incidence of human skin cancer and level of ultraviolet radiation exposure as the latter relates to latitude. Their data on non-melanoma skin cancer frequency among US Caucasians are presented in the table below.

A first-order equation least-squares regression analysis can be performed correlating the logarithm of the annual number of cases with the secant of the latitude. The log transformation is done on the basis of Cutchis (1974) and Reid *et al.* (1976: 179). The secant transformation is done on the basis of the ultra-violet shielding effect of the atmospheric ozone (Cutchis, 1974). No correction is made for altitude on the basis of Caldwell (1968: 251). Although the correlation is weak ($r^2 = 0.70$), the data suggest that there is an average increase of 168 cases per 10^6 year per degree shift toward the equator (that is, 1.51 cases/km) in the latitudinal range of 45° to 30°.

Recently, Scotto *et al.* (1976: 6) have published data on the annual accumulation

Table 1.14. Frequencies of non-melanoma skin cancer among US Caucasians

Location	Latitude	Average altitude (m)	Cases per 10^6 per year
Dallas–Fort Worth Texas	32° 46′ N	170	3790
San Francisco–Oakland California	37° 47′ N	200	1840
[Des Moines] Iowa	41° 35′ N	290	1240
Minneapolis–Saint Paul Minnesota	44° 58′ N	260	1510

Note:
The cancer data are from Scotto *et al.* (1974).

of ultra-violet radiation reportedly in the wavelength range causing erythaema (sunburn), and thus presumably also cancer, for essentially the above four locations. Their data follow (given in units of which about four are said to produce erythaema of typical Caucasian skin): Fort Worth, 16 059; Oakland, 15 086; Des Moines, 12 516; and Minneapolis, 10 650. Unfortunately, a regression analysis comparable to the one done above, in this instance of log of number of cases versus annual ultra-violet exposure, does not show as good a relationship ($r^2 = 0.60$), and this despite a very close correlation between ultra-violet level and secant of latitude ($r^2 = 0.97$).

Thus, although these data suggest a relationship between skin cancer and ultra-violet exposure, they are not by themselves fully convincing.

2. Chemical and biological weapons

Superior numerals, thus [5], *refer to notes on pages 46–48.*

I. Introduction

Chemical warfare refers to the military use of chemical agents for hostile purposes; biological warfare refers to the use of living organisms, usually micro-organisms, for such purposes. The utility of these agents as weapons depends upon their toxicity, pathogenicity or deteriorating abilities.[1] Chemical or biological agents can be directed against enemy personnel, against their livestock or crops, against their natural eco-systems or even against their *matériel*.

In the present chapter are presented a brief history of chemical and biological warfare, descriptions of the agents involved in such warfare and discussions of the ecological consequences of their use. Chemical anti-plant agents are dealt with at length elsewhere (SIPRI, 1976 a) and are therefore not covered here. Nor is the use of larger animals, such as various insects (Ambrose, 1973, 1974; Beck, 1937) and cetaceans (Wallace, 1973), which have been considered for military purposes, since the environmental ramifications are relatively minor.

II. Description

History

Throughout military history, there are numerous minor examples of chemical warfare and even some of biological warfare.[1] However, chemical weapons were not employed on a grand scale until World War I (note 2), and then not again massively until the Second Indochina War. The former instance is outlined below, the latter elsewhere (SIPRI, 1976 a). Fortunately, there has so far been no large-scale use of biological weapons.

During World War I, large quantities of chemical agents of a wide diversity were employed by the several belligerents. No less than 45 agents have been listed: 18 lethal ones (of which 14 were lung agents and

4 were dermal agents) and 27 classed as harassing agents (SIPRI, 1971 a: I). The combined World War I expenditure of these chemicals was well over 100×10^6 kg, with dose rates in some localities that eventually must have exceeded 100 kg/ha.

Among the most heavily used chemicals during World War I were four harassing agents (xylyl bromide, benzyl bromide, bromoacetone and ethyl iodoacetate), four lethal lung agents (chlorine, phosgene, trichloromethyl chloroformate and chloropicrin), and one lethal dermal agent (mustard gas or bis[2-chloroethyl]sulphide). Many of these agents are today obsolete.

There appear to be no studies or even observations of the impact that the World War I chemicals had on the animals or plants of Europe or, indeed, on any of the involved ecosystems. However, their impact on the enmeshed fauna (at least its mammalian component) must have been great, to judge from the enormous human toll taken by these chemicals, despite the evasive and protective measures taken by the combatants. Chemical warfare during World War I is known to have produced 1.3×10^6 casualties, of which 10^5 were fatal. Epstein *et al.* (1969: 71) mention that the regions in question were half a century later in normal and fully productive use. However, only a most detailed examination would reveal any subtle, long-term ecosystem debilitation that might have occurred so long after the fact.

Anti-personnel agents

A wide array of chemical and biological weapons could exist in the military repertoires of at least the major powers (Army and Air Force, 1965, 1967; SIPRI, 1973 b). The anti-personnel agents are covered in the present section, whereas those other than anti-personnel are left to the next one.

The chemical anti-personnel agents are usually separated according to their approximate level of toxicity into 'harassing', 'incapacitating' and 'lethal'. However, the actual level of danger of any particular agent depends upon its manner of application, the concentration employed and the nature or condition of the recipient. The lethal-agent category is usually further divided on the basis of primary physiological action. Thus there are the 'nerve' agents that attack the nervous system, the 'blood' agents that poison the blood, the 'lung' or 'respiratory' agents that asphyxiate, and the 'dermal' or 'cutaneous' agents that blister the skin. The chemical agents of biotic origin (as opposed to those that are synthesized in the laboratory) are generally classed by themselves irrespective of their mode of action.

The biological anti-personnel agents of potential utility are meant for dissemination as live organisms and are most often divided according to their taxonomic position rather than to their degree of toxicity or mode of action. Thus there are assumed to exist a variety of viral, rickettsial, bacterial, fungal and even protozoan agents.

Various factors influence the military usefulness of chemical and biological weapons. Whether or not any one of these factors is considered strategically or tactically favourable depends upon the military and political situations and perhaps also upon one's individual perspective. First of all, despite the wide diversity of known or suspected chemical and biological agents, it appears that most can be formulated for delivery as a gas or else as an aerosol (that is, as a suspension in air of ultra-fine liquid or solid particles). Secondly, overt delivery can be via projectile (grenade, shell, bomb, missile or the like) or via spray equipment (mounted on vehicles, ships or aircraft). Covert delivery by saboteur can take a variety of forms.

It is well within present military capabilities to attack an area hundreds if not thousands of hectares in size. Moreover, the production of at least some of the agents is inexpensive in comparison with alternative weapons of comparable impact. Chemical and biological munitions also weigh less than their conventional counterparts, a factor of some logistical importance. For at least some of the agents, the extent of their production and stockpiling and even of their testing can be kept secret with relative ease.

Among the possible chemical and biological agents there are some for which neither an effective warning system nor an effective system of defence seems feasible. Thus, in addition to their physiological impact, these agents could instill terror in an enemy. Still another attribute to consider is that the action of a number of agents is delayed for hours or even days. Finally, the effectiveness of their delivery and of their potency depend in some instances rather heavily on the prevailing meteorological conditions.

Agents other than anti-personnel

A variety of chemical and biological anti-animal, anti-plant and anti-*matériel* agents can be imagined, and some may have been used. Livestock or other animals could be attacked with a number of presumably available agents.[3] Many of the chemical agents categorized as anti-personnel agents could be employed for this purpose. Even a biological attack on livestock might involve an anti-personnel agent, for example,

Bacillus anthracis (Bacillaceae), discussed below. However, Epstein *et al.* (1969: 46) enumerate 16 biological agents that seem especially suited for use against domestic animals, nine of them viral, two rickettsial, three bacterial and two fungal.

Attacks on an enemy's crops or other vegetation of use to him have, of course, become a matter of recent military history.[4] Biological attacks on crop plants are also feasible. Indeed, Epstein *et al.* (1969: 47) list 13 likely candidates, five viral, three bacterial and five fungal. Their tabulation includes serious diseases of rice (*Oryza sativa;* Gramineae), corn (*Zea mays;* Gramineae), wheat (*Triticum vulgare;* Gramineae) and potato (*Solanum tuberosum;* Solanaceae). Moreover, there appears to be no reason why such economic crops as cotton (*Gossypium hirsutum;* Malvaceae), coffee (*Coffea arabica;* Rubiaceae), rubber (*Hevea brasiliensis;* Euphorbiaceae) or sugar cane (*Saccharum officinarum;* Gramineae) might not also be similarly singled out for destruction.

Although most chemical and biological agents leave an enemy's *matériel* unscathed, some do not. Chemical agents are said to exist that have the purpose of destroying equipment and other artifacts of use to the enemy. Thomas and Thomas (1970: 16) suggest the existence of anti-lubricant agents that would cause equipment to break down (see also Gravel *et al.*, 1971–1972: I:579). Moreover, during the Second Indochina War, the USA is alleged to have disseminated chemicals over North Vietnam for the purpose of fouling up ('attenuating') the radars the enemy used for aiming its defensive surface-to-air missiles (Hersh, 1972). Furthermore, the USA recently admitted to having considered during that war the dropping of emulsifying agents onto unpaved Laotian roads in order to make them impassable (Pell, 1974: 123).

III. Ecological consequences

General

The ecological consequences of chemical or biological warfare can run the gamut from inconsequential to disastrous. Five more or less arbitrarily chosen possibilities are explored below. The first of these cases involves chemical harassing agents and uses 'CS' (*o*-chlorobenzalmalononitrile) as an example, leaning especially upon experience from the Second Indochina War. The remaining four cases are more speculative, since these agents apparently have not yet been employed for hostile military purposes: 'VX' (S-(2-diisopropylaminoethyl) O-ethyl methyl phosphonothiolate) as an example of lethal synthetics; botulinal toxin as an example of naturally occurring lethal chemicals; the bacterium causing anthrax as an example of micro-organisms as biological agents; and the virus causing yellow fever as an example of viruses as biological agents.

In these examples, a whole host of esoteric chemical and bizarre biological possibilities is ignored as well as the synergistic impact that might be achieved from the simultaneous applications of different agents. However, the general nature of the impact of this class of weapons will be suggested by the cases outlined.

Chemical harassing agents

A number of non-lethal, harassing agents are to be found today in the military (and police) arsenals of the world, among them 'CN' or 'mace' (ω-chloroacetophenone), 'DM' or 'adamsite' (10-chloro-5,10-dihydro-phenarsazine), and 'CS' (o-chlorobenzalmalononitrile) (Army and Air Force, 1967). CS in one form or another appears to be the harassing agent of current military preference.[5] It results in militarily significant harassment of unprotected personnel at a particulate aerosol concentration in the atmosphere somewhat above 1 mg/m^3. Used at this level, CS induces intense lacrimation (crying), sternutation (sneezing) and irritation of the upper respiratory tract.

A tactical innovation of the Second Indochina War was the employment by the USA of CS1 (a finely pulverized form of CS) for protracted area denial (Blumenfeld and Meselson, 1971). An especially non-degradable form – CS2 – was developed in 1968 for this use. Whereas the application of CS1 can render an area inhospitable for perhaps 15 days (Army, 1969: 16), that of CS2 will do so for 30 to 45 days (Cannon, 1971: 146). Precise durations depend, of course, on such factors as initial level of application and subsequent rainfall.

Although the US Department of Defense has released no information on US expenditures of CS in Indochina, one can at least gain an indication of their magnitude from the procurement figures available for the war years (Table 2.1). The total quantity of CS overtly procured by the US Department of Defense during this time amounted to about 9×10^6 kg, about four fifths of this in bulk form and the remainder directly incorporated into munitions. About 30 per cent of the total was in the more persistent CS2 form.

Table 2.1. US procurement of CS gas during the Second Indochina War period: a breakdown by type and year

Fiscal year	CS in bulk	CS1 in bulk	CS2 in bulk	CS in munitions	CS1 in munitions	Total
			Quantity of CS procured (10^3 kg)			
1961–62	?	?	0	?	?	?
1962–63	?	?	0	?	?	?
1963–64	102	64	0	106	?	272
1964–65	42	83	0	42	?	167
1965–66	171	552	0	0	4	727
1966–67	198	349	0	797	26	1 371
1967–68	324	1 474	131	350	6	2 284
1968–69	915	73	1 762	351	26	3 127
1969–70	0	161	830	58	13	1 062
1970–71	0	0	0	33	8	41
1971–72	?	?	?	?	?	?
1972–73	?	?	?	?	?	?
Total	**1 753**	**2 755**	**2 723**	**1 737**	**83**	**9 052**

Notes:

(a) As far as possible, the above data are derived from those of Fulbright (1972: 307); values not obtainable from this source are derived to the extent possible from those of Mahon (1969: 124); values not obtainable from either of these sources are derived from those of McCarthy (1969 a: 15765). Amounts of CS contained in the munitions are from the Army (1969: II); amounts not obtainable from this source are derived to the extent possible from the Army (1967); amounts not obtainable from either of these sources are from the US Army (priv. comm., 17 Jun. 1974).

(b) Missing procurement data have not been released by the US Department of Defense.

(c) Information on CS expenditures in Indochina has never been released by the US Department of Defense.

(d) 'CS' is the code name for o-chlorobenzalmalononitrile. 'CS1' refers to a finely pulverized (micronized) form of CS, whereas 'CS2' is a powder that has been treated to make it water-repellent and thus less rapidly degradable under field conditions.

The level of CS application considered necessary by the military to achieve satisfactory area interdiction appears to have fallen somewhere between 1 kg/ha and 10 kg/ha. The quantity procured was therefore sufficient to interdict at one time or another during the course of the war between 1×10^6 ha and 9×10^6 ha of Indochina. Although at least some CS was employed against each of the four Indochinese countries, most of it was expended against South Vietnam, an area of 17×10^6 ha.

It appears reasonable to assume that the CS so liberally applied to the South Vietnamese environment had no major ecological effects inasmuch as none has been reported in the literature. More subtle effects could, of course, have escaped attention. These would hinge upon the toxicity of CS to the various biota exposed to it during the several weeks of the chemical's existence following its field application; and on this subject, a certain amount of information is available. To begin with, it appears that CS harasses and is toxic to the warm-blooded vertebrates at roughly the same levels as for man. For example, Punte *et al.* (1962) found that rats (*Rattus rattus;* Muridae), mice (*Mus musculus;* Muridae) and pigeons (*Columba livia;* Columbidae) were only slightly more resistant than man to CS via inhalation, whereas guinea-pigs (*Cavia porcellus;* Caviidae) and rabbits (*Oryctolagus cuniculus;* Leporidae) were somewhat more sensitive. Chickens (*Gallus gallus;* Phasianidae) are somewhat less irritated by a given level of CS aerosol exposure than are humans. At least the mammalian toxicity of CS is partially attributable to its conversion *in vivo* to cyanide (Frankenberg and Sörbo, 1973).

With respect to CS contamination of the aquatic habitat, Ward (1973) has reported that the common killifish (*Fundulus heteroclitus;* Cyprinodontidae) is killed by 4 g/m^3 in the ambient water (50 per cent mortality within 96 h, i.e., 96 h LC_{50}), and that the duckweed *Wolffia papulifera* (Lemnaceae) is injured by concentrations of 5 g/m^3 and killed by 100 g/m^3, concentrations not likely to be achieved in the field.

CS also appears to be somewhat toxic to terrestrial vegetation, injury to trees having been reported following their exposure during a civil riot-control operation (Cockrell, 1971). Various different compounds chemically related to CS have been reported to have herbicidal, fungicidal, insecticidal or nematocidal properties (Jones, 1972), and these attributes may well be shared to a greater or lesser extent by CS.

There is little doubt that CS causes at least mild and transient ecological perturbation. It is therefore entirely feasible that such ecological debilitation could become a serious concern of the future if chemical area denial were carried out with agents more toxic or more persistent than CS2.

Lethal synthetics

Among the highly poisonous substances that are assumed to be synthesized and stockpiled for use as agents of chemical warfare are phosgene (carbonyl chloride), hydrogen cyanide, mustard gas (bis[2-chloroethyl]-sulphide), 'GB' or 'sarin' (isopropyl methylphosphonofluoridate) and 'VX' (*S*-(2-diisopropylaminoethyl) *O*-ethyl methyl phosphonothiolate). The last is one of a family of extraordinarily lethal organophosphorus compounds – the so-called V agents – stumbled upon by chemists during the mid 1950s in their search for better insecticides (and whose chemical structure has recently been made public (Sidell and Groff, 1974)).[6]

The V agents are singled out for brief discussion since they, and especially VX, are often considered the most important of the lethal synthetic chemical warfare agents. Kaplan *et al.* (1970) have calculated that, depending upon method of dispersal and weather conditions, an area of 400 ha to 4 000 ha could be subjected to a human lethal dose of VX by the 4×10^3 kg payload of a single aircraft. Epstein *et al.* (1969) discuss the possibility of similar chemical attacks covering 5 000 ha or more. Marriott (1969) claims that a single tactical US 'sergeant' missile with a 726 kg payload of VX will produce at least a 33 per cent casualty rate over a target area of 200 ha.

VX and its relatives are said to be essentially colourless, odourless and non-volatile liquids that lend themselves well to military aerosol dispersion. Entry of organophosphorus compounds of this sort is especially hazardous via inhalation (Hartwell and Hayes, 1965), but is also possible and highly dangerous via the skin (Fredricksson, 1961), making protective action most difficult to carry out. Indeed, a dermal application of less than 10 mg of VX is said to be lethal (Kaplan *et al.*, 1970: 40). The primary mode of toxic action of the V agents is the rapid inhibition of the enzyme acetylcholinesterase, essential for the transmission of nerve impulses.

Although very little direct information is available on the V agents, their ecological impact might be similar to that of the organophosphorus insecticides with which they share anti-cholinesterase activity (Fest and Schmidt, 1973). The most important of the commercial organophosphorus insecticides is 'parathion' (*O,O*-diethyl *O-p*-nitrophenyl phosphorothioate). Great precautions must be taken in applying parathion and its relatives in order to avoid medical disasters (Barnes *et al.*, 1957). Indeed, there is much controversy over their routine use in agriculture.

Information available on the organophosphorus insecticides[6] makes it clear that if the nerve agents were used in an attack at levels lethal to personnel, they would simultaneously destroy the other exposed non-human vertebrates. They would also kill many of the invertebrates, particularly various of the arthropods. On the other hand, the exposed vegetation, although it would absorb the agents, would largely be spared, it seems. However, exposed plants would for a time provide a secondary source of contamination for the herbivores feeding on them (Mulla *et al.*, 1966). In fact, it has been reported that vegetation accidentally contaminated with VX continued to be a danger to sheep (*Ovis aries*; Bovidae) for at least three weeks (Boffey, 1968).

Based on what is known from investigations involving parathion and similar organophosphorus insecticides, neither environmental persistence nor ecological (food chain) concentration would be expected to be particular problems with the V agents, particularly in terrestrial ecosystems. Keith (1969), however, suggests that the avian insectivores, at least, would secondarily ingest lethal levels of such agents by preferentially feeding on the readily available dead and weakened arthropods. He is convinced that there is a high incidence of generally unrecognized organophosphorus poisoning of wildlife associated with the use of parathion and similar insecticides. Moreover, the danger to contaminated aquatic habitats might be somewhat higher than to terrestrial ones (Mulla et al., 1966).

It is clear that an attack with V agents, while it probably will not have a long-term residual effect, would result in an immediate zoological catastrophe. This can become a matter of serious concern if the attack extends over hundreds or even thousands of hectares, as well as it might.

Natural toxins

A number of naturally occurring substances are proposed from time to time as candidates for development as agents of chemical warfare. Most of these are antigenic proteins, and they can range in toxicity from temporarily incapacitating to highly lethal.[7]

Botulinal toxin appears to head the list of natural poisons. However, the list also includes the enterotoxins obtained from *Staphylococcus* spp. (Micrococcaceae), ricin (found in castor beans, the fruit of *Ricinus communis* (Euphorbiaceae)), abrin (found in the seeds of the Indian licorice or jequirity bean (*Abrus precatorius*; Fabaceae)), cicutoxin (found in the roots of the European water hemlock (*Cicuta virosa*; Umbelliferae)) and phallin (from the death cup, the basidiomycete *Amanita phalloides* (Agaricaceae)). The toxins or venoms to be obtained from certain snakes (Ophidia), lizards (Sauria), frogs (Ranidae), ticks (Acarida), fish (Pisces) and coelenterates (Cnidaria) (e.g., jelly fish (Schyphozoa) and sea anemones (Actiniaria)) provide additional possibilities. Some of these would seem to lend themselves to biological mass production, while others might have to await means of synthesis before becoming militarily useful. The possible military use of botulinal toxin is briefly elaborated upon below.

Botulinal toxin is well known as the extraordinarily poisonous product of the anaerobic bacterium *Clostridium botulinum* (Bacillaceae), responsible for the acute food poisoning known as botulism.[7] It appears that this neurotoxin (of which at least half a dozen different antigenic groups exist) can be readily produced in large quantities and can be disseminated as an aerosol. Botulinal toxin can gain effective entry not only via the normal oral route, but also through inhalation and subsequent absorption through any mucous membrane. The lethal dose for humans varies with the route of entry, but is of the order of 1 μg or less (some reports suggesting much less).

Botulinal toxin functions by interfering with the release of acetylcholine at the neuromuscular junction, thereby preventing the subsequent contraction of the muscles and thus leading to flaccid paralysis. Without protection or treatment, the mortality rate when the toxin is ingested (that is, from botulinal food poisoning) can be expected to reach 65 per cent; when it is inhaled the mortality rate is likely to be higher. If the toxin is properly stabilized for military dispersion, the area of lethal coverage with a botulinal toxin attack has been estimated by Kaplan *et al.* (1970) to be 1 200 ha per aircraft.

The ecological consequences of a widespread attack with botulinal toxin can only be guessed at from the fragments of available information. The toxin is highly toxic to a number of animals, but man appears to be the most sensitive. From the veterinary literature it becomes clear that botulism is a serious potential problem among chickens (*Gallus gallus*; Phasianidae), game-farm pheasants (*Phasianus colchicus*; Phasianidae) and mink (*Mustela vison*; Mustelidae) raised for their pelts. It is somewhat less of a problem for horses (*Equus caballus*; Equidae), cattle (*Bos taurus*; Bovidae) and sheep (*Ovis aries*; Bovidae); and it is a rare occurrence in swine (*Sus scrofa*; Suidae), dogs (*Canis familiaris*; Canidae) and cats (*Felis catus*; Felidae). In the wild, the birds appear to be particularly susceptible to botulinal mortality, at least 72 avian species being known to succumb to the toxin (Rosen, 1971). One exception, however, is the vulture (*Cathartes aura*; Cathartidae) (M. N. Rosen, Cal. Dept. Fish and Game, priv. comm., 5 Feb. 1974). The most sensitive birds are found among the water fowl and shore birds. Botulism (under the name of limberneck) can be responsible for the death of many thousands of wild ducks (Anatidae) at a time. Finally it is important to mention that botulinal toxin can remain stable in the environment and be a continuing source of danger for as long as a week, particularly under cool, anaerobic conditions such as occur in nonmoving water (Army and Air Force, 1967).

Thus on the face of it, it would seem that a widespread botulinal toxin attack might well wreak havoc within the bird population of the region in question. It would, moreover, selectively remove from it some of the mammals and perhaps other animals, depending upon their innate susceptibility, their feeding habits and other factors. Of course, the impact of such an attack might be even more devastating than has just been suggested. The available literature is based primarily upon the entry of the toxin (in conjunction with the bacterium) via the oral route where, depending upon the species, a greater or lesser amount of digestive detoxication occurs. It is quite conceivable that the virulence of the toxin becomes greatly enhanced for some species – perhaps by more than an order of magnitude – if entry should be gained via the respiratory route (Lamanna, 1961).

Micro-organisms

Various micro-organisms appear to be suitable for use as agents of biological warfare.[8] In addition to the bacteria discussed in the present section and the viruses of the next one, these include such rickettsia as *Rickettsia prowazekii* (Rickettsiaceae) (the cause of typhus) and *Coxiella burnetii* (Rickettsiaceae) (the cause of Q fever), such fungi as *Coccidioides immitis* (Moniliaceae) (the cause of desert fever or coccidioidomycosis) and such protozoa as *Toxoplasma gondii* (Haplosporida) (the cause of toxoplasmosis).

Of the bacteria, up to about a dozen highly virulent species appear to be eminently suitable for biological warfare. The list includes *Pasteurella pestis* (Brucellaceae?) (the cause of plague), *Francisella tularensis* (Brucellaceae?) (the cause of tularemia), *Brucella abortus* (Brucellaceae?) (a cause of undulant fever or brucellosis), *Salmonella typhi* (Enterobacteriaceae) (the cause of typhoid fever) and *Bacillus anthracis* (Bacillaceae) (the cause of anthrax).

The use of *Pasteurella pestis* as an agent of biological warfare may date back to the mid 14th century (Derbes, 1966). Feodosiya (then Kaffa, an important Black Sea port) had been able to withstand a three-year siege, but fell in 1346 shortly after plague-infected cadavers were catapulted over its walls to initiate a decimating plague within.

The highly virulent bacterium *Bacillus anthracis* is the causative agent of the febrile and septicaemic (blood poisoning) disease known as anthrax. This exceedingly infectious disease of most mammals and a variety of other animals is often fatal if left to run its own course (Choquette, 1970). Among the groups that have been experimentally demonstrated to contract the disease are a variety of mammals, birds, amphibians and fish (L. P. E. Choquette, Can. Dept. Environ., priv. comm., 22 Feb. 1974). Normal dissemination is via the bacterial spores, which are transmitted and gain entry in a multiplicity of ways. The pulmonary form of the disease, contracted by spore inhalation, is nearly always rapidly fatal.

The spores of *Bacillus anthracis* are easy to mass-produce, are extraordinarily resistant to the vicissitudes of the environment and lend themselves well to military aerosol dispersion. The inhalation of less than 1 μg of spores provides a lethal dose to humans. Moreover, it is apparently possible to produce mutant forms of *B. anthracis* that do not respond to presently available antibiotic therapy. Calculations by Kaplan *et al.* (1970) suggest that a single aircraft would easily be able to deliver a dose of spores initially lethal to 75 per cent of the humans over an area of perhaps 4 000 ha; Hedén (1967) and Epstein *et al.* (1969) suggest significantly larger areas.

A large-scale attack with *Bacillus anthracis* spores would debilitate if not destroy many of the populations of mammals throughout the attacked region. Moreover, it would have a greater or lesser impact on numerous other animal taxa as well.

Bacillus anthracis appears capable of establishing itself in a wide range of climates. Thus in many parts of the world a biological attack with these bacteria would establish them in the local ecosystems, thereby providing permanent reservoirs of the disease. Occasional outbreaks could be expected to occur from then on. Even in regions not conducive to permanent naturalization, spores in the soil can remain viable and a continuing focus of infection for many years. In fact, Wilson and Russell (1964) found that *B. anthracis* spores can remain alive in soil for at least 60 years (cf. also SIPRI, 1973 b: 131). Even if man were to attempt to undo the results of such an assault on the environment he would find, to quote one authority, that 'the control of anthrax in free-living animals presents many problems, some of them seemingly insurmountable' (Choquette, 1970: 262).

It becomes evident that bacterial warfare could result in significant ecosystem debilitation of indefinite duration.

Viruses

More than a dozen viruses are possible agents of biological warfare.[9] In fact, a virus was employed in one of the few more-or-less well documented instances of biological warfare. During one of the French and Indian wars in the American colonies, the British in 1763 had the admitted intent to spread smallpox virus insidiously among their Indian enemies for the express purpose of debilitating them, and then, so it seems, carried out this scheme (Stearn and Stearn, 1945: 44–45).

Among the less exotic viruses that seem eminently suitable for use as biological agents are those causing yellow fever, dengue fever, Rift

Valley fever and one dangerous disease or another referred to as encephalitis. The different possible viruses range in toxicity from temporarily incapacitating to lethal. Several can be transmitted as an aerosol, whereas others may require military dissemination via an infected vector organism such as a mosquito (Culicidae) or tick (Acarida). The virus that causes yellow fever is singled out for discussion here.

The yellow fever virus (*Flavovirus febricis*) (an arthropod-borne arbovirus in antigenic group B) normally lives and multiplies within certain mosquitoes, most important among them *Aëdes aegypti* (Culicidae) and *Haemogogus* spp. (Culicidae). It is transmitted to man, some other primates and perhaps several further species of warm-blooded vertebrates by these insects when they feed on the blood of their prey. On the other hand, this virus appears to be without effect on reptiles or amphibians (Bugher, 1951: 361, 379–380), nor does it appear to cause any harm to birds (Bugher, 1951: 360–361) or arthropods (R. W. Chamberlain, US Public Health Serv., priv. comm., 9 Apr. 1974).

Yellow fever has been a scourge of mankind for centuries, with occasional epidemics occurring to this day (Burnet and White, 1972: XIX). One such epidemic during 1960 to 1962 killed more than 15×10^3 Ethiopians (Série *et al.*, 1964). The yellow fever fatality rate for unprotected humans is often between 30 and 40 per cent, but goes as high as 85 per cent when the disease is introduced into a virgin area, as it did in the Ethiopian epidemic just mentioned.

The yellow fever virus would seem to make a fine biological warfare agent because of the ease with which large quantities could be prepared in the laboratory, and because it can be disseminated directly to humans as an aerosol, bypassing the militarily cumbersome mosquito (Culicidae) vector. Kaplan *et al.* (1970) estimate that the initial zone of lethal contamination from a yellow fever virus attack would cover an area of 600 ha per aircraft.

A large-scale attack with yellow fever virus in the warmer portions of the world might well establish a permanent new reservoir of the disease. The introduction of this virus into a tropical forest ecosystem would presumably have a significantly adverse effect on the subhuman primates into the indefinite future. Establishing it in Asia via intentional introduction would be a particular tragedy since it has not as yet become established in that part of the world. According to Karstad (1970: 63), once the yellow fever virus has established itself in a tropical forest, it becomes impossible to control either the arthropod vectors or the mammalian host reservoirs.

It seems safe to conclude that the introduction of a virus into a new habitat could have substantial long-term consequences. For example, the spectacular myxomatosis epizootics of recent years that have laid waste rabbit (*Oryctolagus cuniculus*; Leporidae) populations in various parts of the world provide us with a vivid demonstration of how readily and uncontrollably an introduced virus can spread (Fenner and Ratcliffe, 1965).

IV. Conclusion

Chemical and biological weapons have been employed from antiquity to the present and – international agreements and unilateral renunciations notwithstanding – their employment could be repeated in the future. A number of the agents are relatively inexpensive and easy to manufacture, lend themselves to a variety of overt and covert means of delivery and are militarily effective in the sense that they directly or indirectly render an enemy *hors de combat*. Some would claim that there is a sufficiently widespread public revulsion against chemical and biological weapons to prevent the use of the lethal ones, at least. However, Brown (1968) has argued on the basis of an analysis of the World War II experience that this may be a rather ineffectual deterrent (see also SIPRI, 1971 b).

The massive use by the USA of anti-personnel chemicals as well as anti-plant chemicals during the Second Indochina War suggests that these and similar agents would be used in at least the counter-insurgency wars of the future. In fact, a number of laudatory statements were made about these weapons by military authors writing about that war.

Chemical or biological weapons could find a place in other types of future war as well. Some nations may consider them their substitute for nuclear weaponry, perhaps as weapons of aggression, perhaps only for use *in extremis*, when the nation's very existence is at stake. Other nations may use certain of the available weapons because they do not destroy *matériel*, or perhaps in the belief that they are more humane than the conventional alternatives. Larson (1970), a human geneticist, considers it possible that chemical weapons will be developed in the future that possess ethnic or racial specificity (see also SIPRI, 1973 b: 317–319). No suitable biochemical divergences have as yet been discovered, to judge from the open literature (Chern and Beutler, 1975). However, it seems likely that some nation might be tempted to employ such weapons under certain adversary conditions, should they become available.

Some would suggest that the drawbacks of chemical and biological weapons, especially of the latter, outweigh their military attractions (Hjertonsson, 1973; Miettinen, 1974). Thus it is often argued that the more lethal of the agents are simply too inhumane for man to employ against his fellow man. The use of the various non-lethal harassing and temporarily incapacitating agents are decried because, on the one hand, even these can be lethal under various readily visualized circumstances and, on the other, because of the high likelihood of an escalation to the unambiguously lethal agents.

Another potent argument against the use of chemical or biological agents is the relatively uncontrollable and indiscriminate nature of these weapons. Their impact – presumably contrary to desire – is as likely to be felt by the civil as military sectors of the recipient nation. In fact, the vagaries of wind and water currents and of bird and other animal migrations lead to the possibility that their effect would be felt by some neutral third party, or even by the originating power.

The argument against even stockpiling chemical or biological weapons – to provide, for example, a deterrent in kind – is that their availability will eventually lead to their use. Their manufacture, testing and stockpiling have also been opposed on the grounds that accidental releases are possible during these and related operations. Indeed, a number of serious accidents are already on record. These include the so-called Bari incident in 1943, where escaped mustard gas (bis[2-chloroethyl]-sulphide) inadvertently killed over 100 people (Infield, 1971; Saunders, 1967) and the one in 1968 at Skull Valley, Utah where escaped VX gas (*S*-(2-diisopropylaminoethyl) *O*-ethyl methyl phosphonothiolate) inadvertently killed over 4 000 sheep (*Ovis aries;* Bovidae) (Boffey, 1968; Brodine *et al.*, 1969; Dawson, 1969; Hersh, 1968–1969; Reuss, 1969; VanKampen *et al.*, 1969). The release by the US Army of *Serratia marcescens* (Enterobacteriaceae) in California during 1950, apparently in order to test means of disseminating bacterial agents, appears ultimately to have resulted in more than a dozen innocent civilian fatalities (Mills and Drew, 1976: 33; see also Wheat *et al.*, 1951). Conversely, the current development of the so-called binary chemical agents (which do not gain their potency until two relatively harmless components are combined en route to the target) mitigates somewhat the possibility of accidents (Henahan, 1974; Kanegis, 1970–1971; Norman, 1973; Robinson, 1973; 1975; SIPRI, 1973 b: 306–308).

To all of the above arguments against the employment of chemical or biological weapons must be added the potential long-range effects on man and nature of a massive chemical or microbiological intrusion. Neither the magnitude of the immediate effects nor the severity of the ultimate consequences of chemical or biological warfare can be predicted with any measure of confidence (SIPRI, 1971 c; Mayer, 1948). One is thus forced to make the conservative assumption that warfare of this type could result in significant ecological debilitation and is therefore an unacceptable pursuit for this reason as well.

In conclusion, it seems that chemical or biological agents could be considered a weapon of choice by some belligerents for selected tactical or strategic purposes, either singly, in combinations amongst themselves, or in conjunction with other types of weapon. Indeed, a number of the chemical or biological weapons would appear to hold a particular attraction for use against a guerrilla force or other adversary that has only modest medical resources at its command and that is, moreover, unlikely to be able to retaliate in kind.

Notes to Chapter 2

1. The literature on chemical and biological warfare that is openly available deals for the most part with the historical, political, and legal aspects of the subject, to a lesser extent with the military, chemical and medical aspects, and virtually overlooks the biological and ecological aspects.

   Of the available literature, the most important item is the exhaustive study of 20th century chemical and biological warfare by SIPRI (1971–1975). A number of other recent book-length treatments are available, some by military authorities (Brown, 1968; Rosebury, 1949; Rothschild, 1964) and several that have emanated from the civil sector (Clarke, 1968; Cookson and Nottingham, 1969; Hersh, 1968; McCarthy, 1969 b; Thomas and Thomas, 1970). The latter group could be extended through the addition of a number of collections of articles (Alexander et al., 1971; Baudisch et al., 1971; Bulletin of the Atomic Scientists, 1960; Neilands et al., 1972; Ronneberg et al., 1960; Rose, 1969; Scientist and Citizen, 1967). There are many widely scattered brief treatments of the subject, including several that provide interesting historical information (Batten, 1960; Cook, 1971; Derbes, 1966; Kokatnur, 1948; Miles, 1970; Nordenskiöld, 1918; West, 1919) and a number that are bibliographies (Armed Forces Chemical Journal, 1964; Meeker, 1972; Robinson, 1974; Tarr, 1965; Wasan, 1970; Westing, 1974 a) and some others that are noteworthy for one reason or another (Holmberg, 1975; Langer, 1967; Meselson, 1970; Sidel and Goldwyn, 1966; SIPRI, 1974 a).

   The summary by Epstein et al. (1969) particularly as complemented by Kaplan et al. (1970) must be singled out as clearly the best available brief treatments of chemical and biological warfare, and especially so in the present context.

   For specific references to chemical warfare, see note 6; and to biological warfare, see note 8.

2. Although a number of books dealing with chemical warfare as it was waged during World War I appeared in the years immediately following that conflict, the best source to begin with is the review by SIPRI (1971 a). Cook (1971) provides an excellent brief account of the initiation of the use of chemicals in World War I.

3. The literature touching upon chemical anti-animal agents is scarce (Epstein *et al.*, 1969) so that one must rely for this category upon that of the chemical anti-personnel agents.[6]

Biological anti-animal agents are discussed by Epstein *et al.* (1969), the Agricultural Research Service (1961) and the Army and Air Force (1965: VII). Siegmund *et al.* (1973) provide a number of pertinent veterinary summaries. The effects of some of the pertinent micro-organisms on domestic animals are covered by Bruner and Gillespie (1973), and on warm-blooded wildlife by Davis *et al.* (1971) and Davis *et al.* (1970). For information on biological anti-personnel agents, see note 8.

4. Chemical anti-plant warfare is covered elsewhere (SIPRI, 1976 a). For a bibliography on the subject, see Westing (1974 a).

Biological anti-plant agents are discussed by Epstein *et al.* (1969), the Agricultural Research Service (1961) and the Army and Air Force (1965: VIII). For background information on many of the militarily attractive plant diseases, the reader is referred to Horsfall and Dimond (1959–1960), Smith (1973) and Boyce (1961).

5. For a detailed examination of the chemical and physiological properties of 'CS' (*o*-chlorobenzalmalononitrile) and for an introduction to the pertinent literature, see Jones (1972). See also Sanford (1976), SIPRI (1971 a: 185–209; 1973 b: 45–46, etc.). Chemicals agents in general are covered in note 6.

Neilands (1972 a) provides an extensive review of the use of CS by the USA in Indochina, and there are a number of additional sources for such information (Blumenfeld and Meselson, 1971; Blumenthal, 1969; Hersh, 1968: 167–186; SIPRI, 1971 a: 185–209; Rose and Rose, 1972; Verwey, 1977). Military (tactical) evaluations have been favourable (Miller, 1966; Peterkin, 1972; VanRiper, 1972; *Army Digest*, 1968).

CS is often referred to as a gas although this is not the case. It is in fact a solid that is dispersed as an ultra-fine powder (aerosol). When CS is manufactured in finely pulverized (micronized) form it is referred to as CS1, and when the latter in turn is made water-repellent (and thus less rapidly degradable under field conditions), it is known as CS2.

6. There is a considerable literature devoted to chemical warfare and the agents involved, especially if one includes publications covering both chemical and biological agents.[1]

The chemical-agent literature includes items by the Army and Air Force (1967), Health, Education and Welfare (1959 b), Lohs (1974 a, b), Neilands (1973), SIPRI (1973 a; 1975 a, b) and Watkins *et al.* (1968). For literature on 'CS' (*o*-chlorobenzalmalononitrile), see note 5; for literature on toxins, see note 7.

Both the so-called 'G' and 'V' agents are sufficiently similar to the organophosphorus insecticides to permit one to lean upon the literature dealing with this class of compounds. The basic text on the chemistry of the organophosphorus insecticides is by Fest and Schmidt (1973). Their medical toxicology has been summarized by Hayes (1963) and Schumacher (1970); see also Lisella *et al.* (1975–1976). Their veterinary toxicology is covered by Radeleff (1970: VII). Their levels of toxicity for numerous animals have been compiled by Pimentel (1971), Tucker and Crabtree (1970) and Heath *et al.* (1972). Bibliographies relevant in part have been prepared by Fox (1970), Ingram and Tarzwell (1954), Headley and Erickson (1970) and Thomas *et al.* (1964).

7. Some of the more comprehensive recent publications on natural poisons, venoms and toxins are by Ajl *et al.* (1970–1972), Bücherl *et al.* (1968–1971), Halstead (1965–1970), Purchase (1974), Ràsková (1971–1972), Simpson and Curtis (1971–1974), and Vries and Kochva (1971–1973). Moreover, SIPRI (1974 a) has speculated upon the utility of some of these toxins for military purposes.

Specifically with respect to botulinal toxin, excellent reviews have been prepared by Lamanna (1959) and Lamanna and Carr (1967). Holvey *et al.* (1972: 711–714) provide a medical summary for botulinal toxin; Siegmund *et al.* (1973: 345–347, 1083–1084) and Bruner and Gillespie (1973: 368–377) provide veterinary summaries. Rosen (1971) reviews botulism in wild birds.

8. In addition to the literature, that deals with both biological and chemical warfare,[1] there exist a considerable number of useful items dealing specifically with biological weapons, including those by the Agricultural Research Service (1961), Barrairon (1973), Federal Civil Defense Administration (1951), Fothergill (1963), Health, Education and Welfare (1959 a), Hedén (1967), Jenkins (1963), Kaplan (1960), Leitenberg (1967), Mayer (1948), Rosebury (1960) and Rosebury and Kabat (1947). For literature dealing with viruses, see note 9.

   For general medical summaries of the diseases caused by many of the potential biological warfare organisms, the reader is referred to Holvey *et al.* (1972); similarly, for veterinary summaries one can turn to Siegmund *et al.* (1973) and Bruner and Gillespie (1973). Davis and Anderson (1971), Davis *et al.* (1971) and Davis *et al.* (1970) have brought together much pertinent information on infectious and parasitic diseases of wild mammals and birds.

   Specifically with respect to anthrax, Holvey *et al.* (1972: 161–163) provide a medical summary, and Siegmund *et al.* (1973: 328–331) a veterinary summary. Bruner and Gillespie (1973: 344–358) discuss the disease with respect to domestic animals, whereas Choquette (1970) performs this function for wild mammals.

9. The use of viruses in biological warfare is discussed by Epstein *et al.* (1969), Kaplan *et al.* (1970) and SIPRI (1973 b). Medical information on many of the pertinent viruses is summarized by Holvey *et al.* (1972), and veterinary information by Siegmund *et al.* (1973) and Bruner and Gillespie (1973). Their relationships to wildlife are covered in part by Davis *et al.* (1971) and Davis *et al.* (1970). Literature dealing with biological warfare in general is covered in note 8.

   Yellow fever is covered thoroughly by Strode (1951). See also Burnet and White (1972: XIX) and Gillett (1972: 208–223).

3. Geophysical and environmental weapons

Superior numerals, thus [5], refer to notes on pages 62-63.

I. Introduction

Increasing attention is being paid to the manipulation of geophysical or environmental forces for hostile purposes. Some categories of this type of warfare, including the instigation of fires and of floods, have been practised since ancient times. Others, such as rain-making, are in their infancy. And still others are only possibilities for the future.[1]

This chapter describes several of these so-called geophysical or environmental weapons as well as the ecological consequences of their employment. Special emphasis is given to the military use of fire, of floods and of rain-making.

II. Description

General

Geophysical warfare can involve hostile manipulations of the atmosphere, of the land and its associated fresh waters, or of the oceans. The present section touches upon a number of the more speculative possibilities involved. A number of hostile modifications of the atmosphere have been suggested as military possibilities for the future. In addition to the rainfall modification covered below, these include various manipulations of the electrical properties of the ionosphere or troposphere. The purpose of this form of attack would be to interfere with enemy radio, radar or other electromagnetic waves, thereby disrupting enemy communication, remote sensing, navigation and missile guidance systems. Indeed, it appears that some primitive attempts have already been made along these lines. It is reported that during the Second Indochina War the USA attempted to disrupt North Vietnamese radars being used for aiming defensive surface-to-air missiles by introducing undisclosed chemical agents into the troposphere (Hersh, 1972).

If techniques were to be devised for initiating hurricanes or cyclones – or even for only redirecting natural ones – this would make available to the military an immensely destructive force. Moreover, if cloud-to-ground lightning could be controlled, those capable of doing so would finally have achieved a power hitherto reserved for Zeus alone (Ritchie, 1959).

The layer of ozone that envelops the earth within the lower stratosphere is considered to be necessary to shield the earth's biota from harmful amounts of ultra-violet radiation, a subject that was touched upon in Chapter 1. It is perhaps already within our capability to open a 'window' in this ozone layer over an enemy's territory by injecting into it a bromine compound via controlled releases from an orbiting satellite (Sullivan, 1975).

Hostile manipulations of the land that have been suggested as military possibilities of the future seem for the most part to be highly dependent for their success on the local site factors. For example, if an enemy region happens to be tectonically unstable it might become possible to trigger an earthquake there. Similarly, quiescent volcanoes situated in enemy territory could perhaps be stimulated into destructive activity. Some local landforms might well be amenable to disruption through the triggering of avalanches or landslides. And for enemy tundra regions it might be feasible during the summer season to destroy the vegetational ground cover. This would result in a lowering of the level of the permafrost which, in turn, would reduce the trafficability of the area and could result in additional forms of military inconvenience. Land disruption via flooding is covered below.

Among the hostile ocean modifications that have been suggested as military possibilities for the future are physical or chemical manipulations that are meant to disrupt acoustic (sonar) or electromagnetic properties of the attacked waters. Again the purpose for such attack would be the disruption of enemy underwater communication, remote sensing, navigation and missile guidance systems. A second possibility involving the ocean habitat is the generation of tsunamis for the purpose of destroying coastal cities and other nearshore facilities. One way that has been suggested for creating a tsunami on demand is to set off a nuclear device in an appropriate underwater locality (Clark, 1961).

Fire

Through past ages fire has been the most destructive agent available to man. It should thus come as no surprise that fire has long been used in warfare.[2] Its primary use in war has always been for the destruction of man's artifacts, that is, as an anti-*matériel* weapon; its second major use has been as an anti-personnel weapon. However, the present discussion dwells upon widespread military burning in rural areas. There the destruction of vegetation by incendiary means can be used to deny an enemy forest cover, food, feed or industrial crops of one sort or another.

Fire has been used in war since ancient times. During the battles between the Israelites and the Philistines around the 12th century B.C., Samson is recorded as once having destroyed the Philistines' agricultural and horticultural fields by letting loose amongst them several hundred foxes (*Vulpes*; Canidae) whose tails had first been set afire (Judges 15: 3–5). During the first century B.C., in what is now Italy, Lucretius (ca. 55 B.C.: 209) described a huge forest fire, noting that '. . . a fierce conflagration, roaring balefully, has devoured a forest down to the roots and roasted the earth with penetrative fire. . . . The blaze may have been started . . . by men who had employed fire to scare their enemies in some woodland war. . . .'.

From those times to the present, numerous instances can be cited of the hostile use of fire, mostly for anti-*matériel* or anti-personnel purposes.[2] Until the 17th century, however, such incendiary warfare was to some extent limited by the very restricted range of catapults and other delivery systems that were available for incendiary devices. Then, with the rise of artillery, a useful long-range delivery system became available and various more-or-less efficient incendiary shells were developed (Manucy, 1949: 69–70; Fisher, 1946: 110–111). So-called carcasses – hollow, vented iron shells filled with pitch and ignited at the time of firing – made their début in 1672 and were much used for setting military fires for more than two centuries. Then, beginning in the late 18th century, 'hot shot' – iron cannon balls brought to red heat before firing – came into vogue as incendiary missiles. The hot shot was prepared in shot furnaces, which were standard equipment for artillery batteries during the 19th century.

World War I saw the introduction not only of more sophisticated incendiary artillery shells, but also of the first air-delivered incendiary bombs. The use of these weapons during World War I, although rather limited, gave the world a hint of today's massive incendiary warfare. Indeed, fire has been used extensively for military purposes in more recent times and a diversity of highly efficient incendiary weapons and delivery systems can be found today in the major arsenals of the world (SIPRI, 1975 c: II).

Clearly the most spectacular military application for fire in recent times has been in the decimation of cities. During World War II, for example, the USA and its allies aerially attacked several dozen German and Japanese cities with the express intent of destroying them by fire. Indeed, several of these attacks have carved out for themselves permanent niches in military history. These include especially the destruction of Hamburg in August 1943 (Caidin, 1960), of Dresden in February 1945 (Irving, 1963) and of Tokyo in March 1945 (Bond, 1946: 165–167; Craven and Cate, 1953: XX). The incendiary attack on Tokyo was the most destructive in both life and property of any aerial attack throughout World War II, either conventional or nuclear (Craven and Cate, 1953: 617). The destruction of Pyongyang by the USA during the Korean War provides still another notorious example (Futrell *et al.*, 1961: 258). All in all, it is generally recognized in military circles today that the annihilation of cities is accomplished more expeditiously, less expensively, with higher casualties and with greater demoralization of enemy civilians by incendiary attack than by any other conventional means (Björnerstedt *et al.*, 1973; D'Olier *et al.*, 1947).

The incendiary destruction of crops has been practised on a small scale in modern times by the armed forces of a number of nations. During the Second Anglo–Boer War (1899–1902), for example, the Boers set the torch to wide areas of the veldt in order to deny forage to the advancing British (Wet, 1902: 181). The British for their part have destroyed crops both in local, counter-insurgency warfare (in Malaya (Kutger, 1960–1961)) and in general, large-scale warfare (against Germany during World War II (Björnerstedt *et al.*, 1973: 46; SIPRI, 1975 c: 82, 112–113)). The USA fire-bombed enemy crops during the Second Indochina War (Howard, 1972) and considers incendiary attack to be one of the recommended procedures for destroying enemy crops, especially in counter-insurgency warfare (Army, 1967–1970: 69; 1969: 50).

Intentional large-scale forest destruction by fire for military purposes seems to have been tried only rarely in modern times. The Japanese during World War II attempted with little success to set wildfires in the western USA, primarily via balloon-delivered incendiary devices.[3] And then there are the US attempts at burning out large forest tracts during the Second Indochina War, described next.

Incendiary weapons were employed during the Second Indochina War in quantities that far exceeded those of any previous war (SIPRI, 1975 c: I). These included magnesium-encased thermit bombs and grenades, white phosphorus bombs and shells, and napalm bombs and canisters. Their use in this war was confined in large part to close-air-support missions. Intentionally set rural wildfires for purposes of area denial or similar widespread harassment, although attempted on several occasions, were forced by natural circumstances to play only a small role in this conflict.

What seems to have been the militarily most successful wide-area incendiary attack of the Second Indochina War was carried out by the USA in the U Minh forest, a stronghold of their enemy in the Delta region (Military Region IV) of South Vietnam. For several weeks in the spring of 1968 the USA was able through repeated heavy incendiary attacks on the U Minh forest to nurture there some fires of uncertain origin (Time, 1968). In another instance, in the spring of 1971, the USA was reported to have dropped enormous quantities of incendiary devices onto the forest lands around a besieged outpost in west central Kontum province (in Military Region II) (Associated Press, 1971). No evaluation of either of these attacks appears to have been made available.

The most noteworthy instances of rural incendiary attack because of their potential for ecological impact were three major attempts by the USA between 1965 and 1967 to initiate massive forest fires over extensive enemy-controlled areas (Hartmann, 1967; McConnell, 1969–1970; Perry, 1968; Randal, 1967; Reinhold, 1972; Shapley, 1972 b). In each of these cases, a large forest area was prepared by herbicide spraying in order to provide an adequate fuel base of dead leaves and twigs. The first of these attempts, 'Operation Sherwood Forest', was carried out during the spring of 1965 for the aim of destroying the almost 3×10^3 ha Boi Loi woods in south-eastern Tay Ninh province (in War Zone C). Then, during 'Operation Hot Tip' in early 1966, an attempt was made to destroy perhaps 7×10^3 ha of forest in the Chu Pong mountains in north central Pleiku province (in Military Region II). And 'Operation Pink Rose' early in 1967 was intended to destroy almost 8×10^3 ha of forest near Xuan Loc in south central Long Khanh province (in War Zone D).

None of these three carefully planned and executed attempts at initiating self-propagating wild fires was successful despite the herbicidal pretreatments, the massive use of incendiary devices and the sundry technical refinements that were added from one operation to the next. The failures can be attributed to the generally wet conditions (high humidity and/or rainfall) that prevail in the region. The finely divided fuels that are necessary to sustain a forest fire take up too much moisture to support combustion when the ambient relative humidity is above 80 per cent, the usual level that obtains throughout much of Indochina. Additionally, not much litter accumulates on the tropical forest floor as a potential source of fuel; and, finally, Mutch (1970) has suggested that tropical rain forests provide a relatively poor grade of fuel even if permitted to become dry (see also Batchelder and Hirt, 1966).

Flooding

Under specialized site conditions, appropriate military actions can bring about flooding of an area. This could be either intentional or unintentional. For example, one of the ramifications of augmenting the rainfall in a region for one military reason or another might be the instigation or enhancement of flooding. Moreover, the likelihood exists of the incidental enhancement of flooding in conjunction with large-scale military land-clearing operations via, for example, chemical anti-plant agents or Rome ploughs (SIPRI, 1976 a).

Where the geography and the season lend themselves to it, the most straightforward means of producing destructive floods is to destroy existing levees, dikes or dams by one means or another. The first two examples given here of such military flooding were, in fact, both self-inflicted. During the Franco–Dutch War of 1672–1678, the Dutch in June 1672 were partially successful in stopping the forces of Louis XIV from overrunning the Netherlands by cutting dikes to create the so-called Holland Water Line (Baxter, 1966: 72–73; Blok, 1907: 380–381). It should be added that this manoeuver was carried out despite the vehement objections of the peasants of the affected region.

The Second Sino–Japanese War of 1937–1945 provides a far more devastating example of intentional military flooding. In order to curtail the Japanese advance, the Chinese in June 1938 dynamited the Huayuan-kow dike of the Yellow River, near Chengchow. This action resulted in the drowning of several thousand Japanese soldiers and stopped their advance along this front. In the process, however, the flood waters also ravaged major portions of Honan, Anhwei and Kiangsu provinces. Indeed, several million hectares of farm lands were inundated in the process, and their crops and topsoil destroyed. The river was not brought back under control until 1947. In terms of more direct human impact, the flooding inundated some eleven cities and more than four thousand villages. At least several hundred thousand Chinese drowned as a result and several million more were left homeless.[5]

During World War II, the Germans in 1944 intentionally flooded with salt water some 200×10^3 ha of agricultural lands in the Netherlands (Aartsen, 1946; Kolko, 1968). This subsequently induced the Dutch to institute a major research programme in order to develop means for rehabiliting these lands (Dorsman, 1947). By way of further example, the USA in August 1943 bombed dikes in an unsuccessful attempt to flood out the Gia Lam airport of Japanese-occupied Hanoi (Craven and Cate, 1950: 527).

During the Korean War, US forces openly attacked irrigation dams in North Korea (Rees, 1964: 381–382). The purpose of these attacks, according to the US Air Force, was two-fold: on the one hand, they were meant to hinder the production by the enemy of its staple food, rice (*Oryza sativa;* Gramineae); and on the other, they were meant as a warning to future Asian enemies of their vulnerability in this regard (Air University Quarterly Review, 1953–1954). Indeed, the destruction of irrigation dams was considered by the USA to be among the most successful of its air operations of the Korean War (Futrell *et al.*, 1961: 627–628, 637).

During the Second Indochina War, the USA again attacked agriculturally important dams, dikes and seawalls with bombing and shelling especially in North Vietnam (Duffett, 1968: 226–235; Lacoste, 1972; Westing, 1973). However, during these hostilities – despite official acceptability of flooding as a means of war (Army, 1962: 36–38) – the USA denied such attacks. It admitted at most that the damage, if any, was inadvertent or 'collateral' (Gliedman, 1972; Porter, 1972).

Rain-making

Military activities presumably can modify meteorological phenomena either inadvertently or by conscious manipulation. One aspect of the latter possibility – rain-making – is the subject of the present section.[6] Apparently eager to test its procedures in the field, or perhaps to show them off, the US Department of Defense has openly attempted (with greater or lesser success) to augment rainfall for civil purposes in such diverse locales as India in 1967, Florida in 1968 and 1970, the Philippines in 1969, Okinawa, Midway and Texas in 1971, and the Azores and California in 1972. Its rain-making and related activities in Indochina, on the other hand, were conducted with great attempts at secrecy.

Beginning in 1963 and continuing at least into 1972, first the US Central Intelligence Agency and then the military carried out extensive attempts to manipulate the rainfall in Indochina. Although all of the countries enmeshed in the Second Indochina War were at one time or another subjected to rain-making attack, it was Laos that bore the brunt of these activities (Table 3.1). The seeding agents employed included silver iodide and lead iodide.

The major reason for the rain-making efforts was reported to be the interdiction of enemy lines of communication, especially the supply routes in south-eastern Laos. Attempts were made each year between

Table 3.1. US cloud seeding operations in the Second Indochina War: a breakdown by year and region

Year	Seeding cartridges expended					Total sorties flown
	South Vietnam	North Vietnam	Cambodia	Laos	**Total**	
1961	0	0	0	0	**0**	0
1962	0	0	0	0	**0**	0
1963	Several	0	0	0	**Several**	Several
1964	?	?	?	?	**?**	?
1965	?	?	?	?	**?**	?
1966	0	0	0	560?	**560?**	56
1967	Several	1 017	0	5 553	**6 570**	591
1968	0	98	0	7 322	**7 420**	734?
1969	0	0	0	9 457	**9 457**	528
1970	0	0	0	8 312	**8 312**	277
1971	0	0	0	11 288	**11 288**	333
1972	1 000?	0	1 000?	2 362?	**4 362**	139
1973	0	0	0	0	**0**	0
Total	**1 000?**	**1 115**	**1 000?**	**44 854?**	**47 969?**	**2 658**

Notes:
(a) The data are from Pell (1974: 92–102) except for the 1963 information, which is from Hersh (1972) and Shapley (1974).

(b) Most of the seeding cartridges used generated either a silver iodide or lead iodide particulate aerosol (Pell, 1974: 91). It appears that the devices used were similar to the commercially available 'Weathercord' (Weather Engineering Corp., Dorval, Quebec), which contains 518 mg of silver iodide (Goyer et al., 1966).

1966 and 1972 to intensify and prolong the annual rainy season in order to make the so-called Ho Chi Minh trail sufficiently muddy to render it impassable, or at least more difficult to use. There were also some unsuccessful attempts (apparently by the Central Intelligence Agency) to achieve a similar result by the aerial application of undisclosed chemical agents with emulsifying action (Pell, 1974: 123). As already mentioned, cloud-seeding in North Vietnam (again with undisclosed chemicals) may have been carried out largely to make inoperable the enemy radars used for aiming defensive surface-to-air missiles (Hersh, 1972). Other reported uses in Indochina included the production of sufficiently bad weather to hamper enemy offensives, the altering of rainfall patterns to aid US bombing missions, the providing of inclement weather to enable the success of covert ground operations, the creation of generally disruptive floods, and the diversion of enemy manpower to undoing the mischief caused by the bad weather instigated.

Although the military seemed satisfied with the level of success of its weather modification operations in Indochina (Gravel *et al.*, 1971–1972: IV:421; Pell, 1974: 103–108), a dispassionate arbiter might be hard pressed to recognize the basis for this satisfaction.

III. Ecological consequences

Fire

Fire has always been a natural factor more or less importantly involved in the shaping of terrestrial ecosystems.[4] Since the beginning of time, there have been innumerable lightning fires. And wherever man has lived, from antiquity to the present, he has continued to set fires, either by accident or design. For a variety of meteorological and other reasons, the frequency and severity of wild fires differ from region to region, running the gamut from common and extensive to virtually non-existent. In the regions of relatively high frequency, fire is in fact the dominant factor determining vegetational (and thus also faunal) composition (Ahlgren and Ahlgren, 1960; Cooper, 1961), irrespective of latitude. Thus, Lutz (1956) has shown that the vegetation characteristic of interior Alaska is determined by the periodic fires that have always been common to that region. Moreover, certain forms of grasslands have become established and perpetuated only through the action of repeated fires, both in temperate zones (Sauer, 1950; Wells, 1965) and in the tropics (Budowski, 1956; Holmes, 1951; Wharton, 1966; 1968).

One might suggest that, as a general rule, the ease with which wild fires can be set and sustained in any particular region is directly correlated with the ability of the natural local ecosystems to survive such assault. The plants indigenous to fire-prone regions have presumably evolved fire survival mechanisms and, in some instances, have even come to depend upon periodic fires in one way or another. Conversely, those plants found in a region rarely subjected to fire are likely to be decimated by a conflagration.

For the many regions throughout the world where natural wildfires are an occasional occurrence, a forest fire is relatively easy to set (at least at certain seasons of the year) and will result in varying amounts of ecological damage. In such a region, a forest fire will injure many of the large trees and kill some of them. The degree of initial damage depends upon the weather conditions at the time of the fire and upon the species of trees involved. The ability of a species to withstand fire damage is, for all but young individuals, to a great extent a function of its bark characteristics, mainly the thickness. Seedlings and saplings are, of course, more highly susceptible to initial damage than larger trees. However, the greatest amount of damage to the trees is caused by the fungi that gain entry via fire wounds (Stickel and Marco, 1936; Hawley and Stickel, 1948: III), and to a lesser extent the insects that do so (Hodges and Pickard, 1971).

Major forest fires can also do a certain amount of harm to the eco-system by damaging the soil. An important source of soil damage is a reduction in the amount of soil litter (that is, of the soil's A_0 horizon). Some litter will burn in the fire (with an associated loss of volatile nitrogen (DeBell and Ralston, 1970; Knight, 1966)), but the greatest ultimate loss is the result of a subsequent diminution of the replenishment of routine losses. Litter with its associated humus is a particularly scarce commodity in the tropics.

With a reduced layer of protective litter, the soil becomes subject to increased erosion and associated problems (Arend, 1941; Lowdermilk, 1930). The loss of nutrients in solution (that is, nutrient dumping) will be a particular problem, perhaps especially the loss of soluble phosphorus (McColl and Grigal, 1975) and soluble potassium (Allen, 1964). Moreover, flood danger will be enhanced.

Fires can also play havoc with the wildlife in an area, both directly and indirectly. However, the degree of damage to any particular species can differ markedly depending upon the season of the year. The direct faunal destruction that is likely to occur as a result of a wild fire has been vividly described by Kipp (1931). Fires are, of course, harmful to animals indirectly via destruction of their food and cover. Moreover, the very different habitat that is likely to develop following a major fire, that is, following vegetational recolonization, will support a new and far less diversified animal community.

Rain-making

One can begin an examination of rain-making with the cloud-seeding agents themselves.[7] Thus, silver iodide and lead iodide (two of the most commonly used agents) can exert at least a minor adverse effect on the ecosystems into which they are introduced (Cooper and Jolly, 1970). Certain aquatic biota such as algae, invertebrates and some fish are the most likely organisms to be harmed by these poisons.

With rainfall augmentation, there is also the possibility of enhanced flood damage. With respect to the Second Indochina War, it remains unknown whether the serious flooding that occurred in North Vietnam in 1971 (Darcourt, 1971; *Vietnam Newsletter*, 1971) can be attributed at least in part to the US attempts at weather manipulation. Indeed, 1971 was the peak year of US cloud-seeding activity (Table 3.1). Even if the seeding was carried out only in Laos, as announced, the prevailing winds during the rainy (cloud-seeding) season are south-westerly, that is, from Laos to North Vietnam. Still another problem associated with increased rainfall would be an enhancement of erosional damage, particularly in hilly terrain and especially when the ground has been previously disrupted by bombing or other hostile activity.

Rainfall manipulation, unless carried out with consistent success over a period of years, would have little obvious effect on most of the plants and animals involved. However, water-dependent insects would be favoured in times of increased rainfall. Since this category of fauna includes a number of important disease vectors, there might be subsequent increases in the incidence of various diseases of wildlife, livestock and humans (Chapter 1, note 12). Indeed, enhanced rainfall could in this and other ways trigger a variety of more-or-less subtle imbalances in the ecosystems being thus tampered with, traceable to the resultant changes in reproductive, growth or mortality rates of some biota. Although such effects are apt to be most pronounced among the lower plants and animals, they are by no means restricted to such forms. For example, the population level of jack-rabbits (*Lepus californicus melanotis*; Leporidae) in Kansas in any particular year is closely correlated with the amount of rainfall during that year (Bronson and Tiemeier, 1959). Moreover, from observations along the coast of Georgia, it is known that a modest shift to an earlier date for the normal autumn rainfall can spell the difference between survival and death for the eggs of the Atlantic loggerhead turtle (*Caretta caretta caretta*; Cheloniidae) (Ragotzkie, 1959).

When rain-making is successful in one area, this may have been at the expense of rainfall diminution in another area, where drought-associated problems could manifest themselves.

Thus, one can safely conclude that seemingly minor changes in precipitation (or in insolation or temperature) could bring about substantial and unexpected changes in the affected ecosystems, both natural and agricultural.

IV. Conclusion

Geophysical or environmental warfare is for the most part still in its infancy. However, its future growth and development appear assured, hinging only upon the continued discovery and refinement of appropriate techniques. As one spokesman for the US Department of Defense admitted in explaining the activities of the Geophysics Group at the US Naval Ordnance Test Station in California, 'Primarily the work is aimed at giving the . . . armed forces . . . the capability of modifying the environment, to their own advantage, or to the disadvantage of an enemy. We regard the weather as a weapon. Anything one can use to get his way is a weapon and the weather is as good a one as any' (Magnuson, 1966: 33).

The human impact of geophysical warfare can range from inconsequential to disastrous, depending upon the techniques employed, the success with which they are employed, the location and duration of their employment and other factors. Moreover, the social impact of hurricanes, earthquakes, lava flows, tidal waves and so forth would be tremendous, should their manipulation become feasible techniques of geophysical warfare.

Rural wildfires initiated by military action could cause a host of severe economic and other social problems, both intentional and unintentional. Even under the best of peaceful conditions, a large rural wildfire can all but overwhelm local efforts to bring it under control, as described in the dramatic account by Holbrook (1943) of some of the major US forest fires of the past and in the gripping fictional, though technically accurate, description by Stewart (1948) of one such fire. In time of war, with the employment of delayed action incendiary devices and scattered anti-personnel mines, the task of fighting a wildfire could become virtually impossible and the fire might have to be left to run its course.

Fires set for hostile purposes can destroy merchantable timber, food crops, rubber plantations and all sorts of other industrial plants, both herbaceous and woody. There can be losses of livestock, buildings and other property. Human lives can be lost as well, even with rural fires. The smoke from the fires contributes to the regional air pollution, with the particulates and some of the hydrocarbons thus generated having both economic and public health ramifications (Hall, 1972; Murphy et al., 1970).

There exists ample civil experience to support the contention that large-scale rural wildfires can be ecologically debilitating and economically devastating. When such fires are of military origin, they are likely to be more damaging than seemingly comparable rural wildfires of non-military origin (even those maliciously set by arsonists). Not only will the military fires be likely to have been initiated and maintained by the massive and repeated applications of highly efficient incendiary devices, but efforts to extinguish them are likely to be hampered by concomitant military actions of various sorts.

The military fires attempted in Indochina were of only minor ecological import owing to the inappropriate regional site conditions. However, if an area not normally subject to natural fires can be ignited by improved incendiary techniques, including appropriate chemical pretreatment, then the ecological impact could be a very serious one. Indeed, pretreatment of the sort just suggested is a technology already under development (Bentley et al., 1971; Bentley and Graham, 1976; Forman and Longacre, 1969–1970; Philpot and Mutch, 1968).

Napalm and other incendiary weapons can be opposed not only on ecological grounds, but on humanitarian grounds as well (Björner-stedt et al., 1973; Red Cross, 1973; SIPRI, 1972; 1975 c; Wulff et al., 1973).

Flooding for hostile purposes can result in enormous agricultural losses, both immediate and delayed, as was shown so well by the Germans in the Netherlands during World War II and the Chinese during the Second Sino–Japanese War of 1937–1945. That the direct human losses can be staggering was also demonstrated by the latter instance. Enhanced rainfall in areas where malaria is prevalent can lead to immediate increases in the incidence of this disease, owing to the improved habitat conditions for the vector insect (Sargent and Tromp, 1964). A number of other diseases follow a similar course. The health and other effects associated with depletion of the ozone layer in the lower stratosphere were discussed in Chapter 1.

It is thus evident that geophysical or environmental warfare is objectional on several levels. Even with optimistic expectations regarding future refinements in technique, the outcome of geophysical modifications for hostile purposes is likely to be unpredictable in magnitude, spatial confinement, side effects and duration. Thus, the intended effects of such military activities cannot be brought to bear on an enemy without the likelihood of an even greater effect on the regional civil populace, to say nothing of the impact on the regional ecology. A further objection that has been raised on occasion is that some of the techniques of geophysical warfare lend themselves readily to covert application, even during times of ostensible peace. In short, geophysical or environmental manipulations for military purposes might well result in a host of severe ecological and social problems, both immediate and delayed.

Notes to Chapter 3

1. The directions that geophysical and environmental warfare might take in the future have been considered by Barnaby (1975; 1976), Canada (1975), Fedorov (1975), Goldblat (1975), Hecht (1976), Israelyan (1974), Jasani (1975), MacDonald (1968), Schneider (1976), Weiss (1974; 1975) and others. For the special case of military incendiarism, see note 2; and for that of military weather modification, see note 6.

   Weather modification and other geophysical changes associated with nuclear warfare are covered in Chapter 1. For references to weather changes brought about by nuclear war, see Chapter 1, note 9.

2. The thesis that fire was the first great force available to man is reviewed by Stewart (1956). Partington (1960) covers in part the military use of fire in ancient times and Fisher (1946) provides a text on incendiary warfare that includes a brief history of the subject from 60 B.C. to 1945 (Chapter VIII). The use of fire during World War II, primarily for the destruction of cities, has been analysed by D'Olier et al. (1947) and by Bond (1946) via a collection of articles. A considerable number of brief accounts of incendiary warfare exist, among them those by Heon (1964), Miller (1958), Lohs (1973) and Sorensen (1948–1949). Certain aspects of incendiary weapon technology have been described by Watkins et al. (1968: Pt. II).

   Björnerstedt et al. (1973) provide an excellent brief over-all treatment of incendiary warfare. The best single major source of information on the subject is the recent monograph by SIPRI (1975 c). Both Björnerstedt et al. and SIPRI emphasize the anti-personnel and anti-matériel aspects of incendiary weapons and the social ramifications of their use.

   Incendiary weapons and techniques of the Second Indochina War have been treated by SIPRI (1975 c: 49–63), Shapley (1972 b), Neilands (1970; 1972 b; 1973) and Takman (1967) (with napalm the major focus for the latter two authors). There also exist a number of secret reports on the subject (Forest Service, 1966; 1970; Kusterer, 1966).

   For a discussion of fires associated with nuclear warfare, see Chapter 1: for references to the subject, see Chapter 1, note 6.

3. During World War II the Japanese repeatedly attempted to initiate large-scale forest fires in the western USA as a means of disrupting the US war effort. There was at least one direct fire-bomb air attack against Oregon (Fujita and Harrington, 1961; Goldenson and Danner, 1948; Holbrook, 1944–1945; Webber, 1975: VI–VII). However, the project was carried out primarily via the release of many thousands of large long-range wind-borne balloons carrying incendiary devices (Conley, 1967–1968; Goldenson and Danner, 1948; Mikesh, 1973; Rahm, 1946; Webber, 1975: X–XI; Wilbur, 1950; Winters, 1974: 296).

4. For a comprehensive coverage of wild fires from the standpoint of forestry, see Brown and Davis (1973). The ecological effects of forest and other wild fires have been reviewed by Ahlgren and Ahlgren (1960), Broido (1963), Cooper (1961), Kozlowski and Ahlgren (1974), Lutz (1956), Mobley (1974) and others. A number of relevant bibliographies also exist (Cushwa, 1968; Hare, 1961; Baker, 1975).

5. The various reports on the June 1938 flooding of the Yellow River do not all agree as to the details of the case. The information provided in the text has been pieced together and averaged from the following sources (chosen for their opposing biases): Boyle (1972: 187), Dorn (1974: 177–178), Freeberne (1973: 68–69), Hsu and Chang (1972: 235), Mossdorf (1941: 150–152), Smedley (1943: 221) and Todd (1942: 205, 207, 224).

This destruction of the Huayuankow dike by the Chinese Kuo-min-tang seems to have resulted in more deaths than any other single human action in history. Indeed, some estimates of the total number of resultant drownings approach the million mark (Boyle, 1972: 187; Freeberne, 1973: 69), although the more conservative estimate of 'several hundred thousand' is used in the text. The three closest rivals to this fatality record appear to be the Allied fire bombing of Dresden in February 1945, with an estimated 135×10^3 fatalities (Björnerstedt et al., 1973: 45); the US fire bombing of Tokyo in March 1945, with an estimated 83×10^3 fatalities (Björnerstedt et al., 1973: 46); and the US atomic bombing of Hiroshima in August 1945, with a conservatively estimated 78×10^3 fatalities (Vellodi et al., 1968: 3).

According to H. Bielenstein (Columbia Univ., priv. comm., 16 Jan. 1976), the military destruction in 1938 of the Yellow River containment system was, in fact, a repetition of a similar event that occurred between A.D. 2 and 11. The earlier catastrophe resulted in a great migration of displaced people to the south, as well as in the fall of a dynasty.

6. The literature dealing with intentional weather modification for civil purposes has been compiled in extenso (Grimes, 1972; Taborsky and Thuronyi, 1960; 1962; Thuronyi, 1963; 1964). See also Hess (1974). Weather modification for military purposes has been discussed on several occasions (Kotsch, 1968; Pell, 1972; Studer, 1968–1969; see also note 1).

The best sources of information on military weather manipulation by the USA in Indochina are a series of US Senate documents (Pell, 1972; 1973; 1974). A number of news accounts and articles on the subject have also appeared (Andersson, 1971; Begishev, 1972; Cohn, 1972; Gliedman, 1972: V, etc.; Greenberg, 1972; Hersh, 1972; Horton, 1976; Norman, 1974; Ognibene, 1972; Purrett, 1972; Recherche, 1972; Shapley, 1972 a; 1974), of which those by Granville (1975) and MacDonald (1975–1976) can be singled out.

7. A number of articles explore the ecological consequences of weather modification for civil purposes, among them those by Cooper and Jolly (1969), Livingstone et al. (1966), Sargent (1967), Waggoner (1966) and Whittaker (1967). These reviews deal primarily with the potential ramifications of rainfall manipulation over extended periods of time. All of the authors agree that the potential ecological impact of such activities is likely to be undesirable, despite the good intentions involved.

The influence on ecosystems of sustained minor differences in temperature is covered in Chapter 1, note 11. The influence on agricultural ecosystems of minor changes in temperature or precipitation is covered in Chapter 1, note 12. References to the influence of minor weather changes on the incidence of bacterial, fungal and insect attacks are provided in Chapter 1, note 12 as well.

4. Epilogue

Nuclear or other weapons of mass destruction are today available to numerous nations. The variety and sophistication of these gruesome weapons and their delivery systems continue to increase as do the number of nations to whom they are available. Local wars continue to occur in different regions of the world and the possibility of another global war remains ever present. Given the capability, the belligerents in any war of the future are certain at least to consider using weapons of mass destruction – weapons that have a devastating impact on both man and nature.

On the other hand, it must be recalled that nuclear weapons have not been exploded for hostile purposes for the three decades since World War II, that lethal chemical weapons have not been employed on a large scale for the six decades since World War I, and that biological weapons have never been used on a significant scale. Although chemical harassing agents and chemical anti-plant agents have both been massively employed within the past decade, during the Second Indochina War, their future employment in this fashion has recently been renounced by the USA.

Moreover, there exists a number of multilateral (though far from universal) treaties that include restrictions of one sort or another on the use of weapons of mass destruction.[1] The use or possession of nuclear weapons has been curtailed in several direct of indirect fashions. For example, about 20 Latin American nations (in concert with the USA, the UK, France and China) have agreed to denuclearize approximately 40 per cent of the land area of the Western Hemisphere south of the USA. The World War II peace treaties imposed prohibitions on the possession of nuclear weapons upon most of the defeated nations. Nineteen or more nations (including the USA, the USSR, the UK and France) have agreed to keep Antarctica free of nuclear weapons; at least 62 nations (including the USA, the USSR and the UK) have similarly agreed to keep most of the ocean floor nuclear-free; and about 74 nations (including the USA, the USSR and the UK) have agreed not to station nuclear weapons on the Moon or elsewhere in outer space. Moreover, more than 100 presently non-nuclear nations have agreed to refrain from possessing nuclear weapons. A conglomerate of additional treaties has restricted the ratifying parties in various ways with respect to the testing of nuclear weapons and to their delivery systems.

Some 96 nations have agreed not to use chemical or biological weapons in war. Most of the defeated nations of World War II agreed, in conjunction with their peace treaties, not to possess chemical or biological weapons. And 73 or more nations have agreed not to produce or stockpile either biological weapons or chemical toxin weapons of biological or other origin. Finally, a number of international treaties that would restrict various weapons of mass destruction are currently under negotiation or open for signature.

It can be seen that the desultory international arms control and disarmament negotiations of the past century have resulted in a hodge-podge of fragmentary controls over weapons of mass destruction and that these have gained only partial acceptance. There thus remains an urgent need for a comprehensive and widely accepted ban on the possession and use of nuclear and other weapons of mass destruction. To single out these weapons is to some extent simplistic inasmuch as the achievement of a peaceful and disarmed world represents an enormously complex and multifaceted problem. However, weapons of mass destruction are especially pernicious because their impact simply cannot be confined either to the target area or to the time of attack. In addition to this inability to contain these means of war to either the spatial or temporal boundaries of attack, they are further repulsive because of their partially unpredictable ramifications and because their impact as a rule does not discriminate between combatants and non-combatants. They must as well be condemned because they wreak havoc within the enmeshed ecosystems.

Ecological considerations have not played a dominant rôle in man's past affairs, whether civil or military. To the extent that such considerations did, in fact, intrude upon his decision-making processes, man simply took for granted a position of dominance in the natural global hierarchy. The validity of this supremacy has, however, never been put to an adequate test. To date, even the most severe anthropogenic perturbations of the global ecosystem have been modest and transitory. However, man has finally attained the technological capabilities to do much more than this. It thus remains to be seen whether he will use these capabilities for military purposes, actions that could lead to a Carthaginian peace that is worldwide in scope.

Note to Chapter 4

1. Treaties that place restrictions on weapons of mass destruction have been compiled by the ACDA (1975), Dupuy and Hammerman (1973), Friedman (1972), Kristoferson

(1975), Schindler and Toman (1972) and others. The law of war as it applies to weapons of mass destruction has been analysed by SIPRI (1976 b). See also the briefer treatments by Barnaby (1976), Blix (1974), Goldblat (1975; 1977), Schneider (1976), Thorsson (1975) and Westing (1974 b). Moreover, the section on arms control and disarmament in each of the *SIPRI Yearbooks* is an especially useful source of pertinent information.

References

Aartsen, J. P. van, 1946. Consequences of the war on agriculture in the Netherlands. *Int. Rev. Agric.*, **37**: 5S–34S, 49S–70S, 108S–123S.

ACDA (Arms Control and Disarmament Agency, US), 1975. Arms control and disarmament agreements: texts and history of negotiations. ACDA Publication No. 77, 159 pp.

ACDA (Arms Control and Disarmament Agency, US), [n.d., 1975?]. Worldwide effects of nuclear war: some perspectives. ACDA, 24 pp.

Agricultural Research Service, US, 1961. Leader's guide to agriculture's defense against biological warfare and other outbreaks: a technical presentation. Special Report No. ARS 22-75. 15 pp.

Ahlgren, I. F. and Ahlgren, C. E., 1960. Ecological effects of forest fires. *Botanical Review*, **26**: 483–533.

Ahmed, A. K., 1975. Unshielding the sun: human effects. *Environment*, **17**(3): 6–14.

Air University Quarterly Review, 1953–1954. Attack on the irrigation dams in North Korea. *Air Univ. Quart. Rev.* (now *Air Univ. Rev.*), **6**(4): 40–61.

Ajl, S. J. *et al.* (eds), 1970–1972. *Microbial Toxins* (Academic Press, New York) 8 vols. [3 821 pp.].

Alexander, A. S. *et al.*, 1971. *Control of Chemical and Biological Weapons.* (Carnegie Endowment for International Peace, New York) 130 pp.

Allen, S. E., 1964. Chemical aspects of heather burning. *J. Applied Ecology*, **1**: 347–367.

Allred, D. M., Beck, D. E. and Jorgensen, C. D., 1965. Summary of the ecological effects of nuclear testing on native animals at the Nevada test site. *Proceedings of the Utah Academy of Sciences, Arts and Letters*, **44**: 252–60.

Ambrose, J. T., 1973. Bees and warfare. *Gleanings in Bee Culture*, **101**(11): 343–345, 364.

Ambrose, J. T., 1974. Insects in warfare. *Army*, **24**(12): 33–38.

Anderson, J., 1971. Air Force turns rainmaker in Laos. *Washington Post* (18 March 1971) p. F7.

Arena, V., 1971. *Ionizing Radiation and Life.* (C. V. Mosby, St. Louis) 543 pp.

Arend, J. L., 1941. Infiltration rates of forest soils in the Missouri Ozarks is affected by woods burning and litter removal. *J. Forestry*, **39**: 726–8.

Armed Forces Chemical Journal, 1964. Chemical warfare bibliography 1957–1963. *Armed Forces Chem. J.* (now *Natl Defense*), **18**(1): 29.

Army, US Dept. of the, 1962. *Barriers and Denial Operations.* US Dept. Army Field Manual No. 31-10, 128 pp.

Army, US Dept. of the, 1967. *Chemical Reference Handbook.* US Dept. Army Field Manual No. 3-8, 132 pp.

Army, US Dept. of the, 1967–1970. *Counterguerrilla Operations.* US Dept. Army Field Manual No. 31-16, 164 + 17 + 18 pp.

Army, U.S. Dept. of the, 1969. *Employment of Riot Control Agents, Flame, Smoke, Antiplant Agents and Personnel Detectors in Counterguerrilla Operations.* US Dept. Army Training Circ. No. 3-16, 85 pp.

Army and Air Force, US Depts of the, 1965. *Military Biology and Biological Agents.* US Dept. Army Technical Manual No. 3-216, 104 + 3 pp.

Army and Air Force, US Depts of the, 1967. *Military Chemistry and Chemical Agents.* US Dept. Army Technical Manual No. 3-215, 101 + 9 + 7 pp. + 2 tables.

Army Digest, 1968. Silent weapons: role of chemicals in lower case warfare. *Army Digest* (now *Soldiers*), **23**(11): 6–11.

Aronow, S., Ervin, F. R. and Sidel, V. W. (eds), 1963. *Fallen Sky: Medical Consequences of Thermonuclear War.* (Hill & Wang, New York), 134 pp.

Associated Press, 1971. Besieged fire base fights off attack by Hanoi commandos. *New York Times* (10 April 1971), p. 7.

Auerbach, S. I., 1968. Postattack insect problems. In National Academy of Sciences *et al.* (eds), *Postattack Recovery from Nuclear War.* (National Academy of Sciences, Washington), 434 pp.: pp. 137–142.

Ayres, R. U., 1965. Environmental effects of nuclear weapons, Rept. No. HI-518-RR. (Hudson Inst, Croton-on-Hudson, N.Y.) 3 Vols. [392 pp.].

Baker, J. O. Jr, 1975. *Selected and Annotated Bibliography for Wilderness Fire Managers.* US Forest Service, 36 pp.

Barnaby, F., 1975. Spread of the capability to do violence: an introduction to environmental warfare. *Ambio*, **4**: 178–85.

Barnaby, F., 1976. Environmental warfare. *Bull. Atomic Scientists*, **32**(5): 36–43.

Barnes, J. M., Hayes, W. J. and Kay, K., 1957. Control of health hazards likely to arise from the use of organo-phosphorus insecticides in vector control. *Bull. World Health Org.*, **16**: 41–61.

Barrairon, P., 1973. [The biological weapon: myth or reality?] *Défense Nationale*, **29**(Aug.–Sep.): 129–142. In French.

Batchelder, R. B. and Hirt, H. F., 1966. *Fire in Tropical Forests and Grasslands.* Rept No. ES-23. US Army Natick Labs, Earth Sciences Div., Natick, Mass., 380 pp.

Batten, E. S., 1966. *Effects of Nuclear War on the Weather and Climate.* Memo. No. RM-4989-TAB. Rand Corp., Santa Monica, Cal., 59 pp.

Batten, J. K., 1960. Chemical warfare in history. *Armed Forces Chem. J.* (now *National Defense*), **14**(2): 16–17, 32.

Baudisch, K., Förster, S., Helbing, H. and Stulz, P. (eds), 1971. *ABC Weapons, Disarmament and the Responsibility of Scientists.* World Federation of Scientific Workers, London, 224 pp.

Bauer, E. and Gilmore, F. R., 1965. Effect of atmospheric nuclear explosions on total ozone. *Reviews of Geophysical and Space Physics*, **13**: 451–8.

Baxter, S. B., 1966. *William III and the Defense of European Liberty 1650–1702.* (Harcourt, Brace & World, New York)., 462 pp. + 8 pl.

Beck, B. F., 1937. Bees as strategists and warriors. *Gleanings in Bee Culture*, **65**: 534–7, 580.

Begishev, V., 1972. Another genocide weapon. *New Times*, **1972**(32): 26–27.

Bensen, D. W. and Sparrow, A. H. (eds), 1971. *Survival of Food Crops and Livestock in the Event of Nuclear War.* Symposium Series No. 24. (US Atomic Energy Commission), 745 pp.

Bentley, J. R., Conrad, C. E. and Schimke, H. E., 1971. *Burning Trials in Shrubby Vegetation Desiccated with Herbicides.* Research Note No. PSW-241. (US Forest Service), 9 pp.

Bentley, J. R. and Graham, C. A., 1976. *Applying Herbicides to Desiccate Manzanita Brushfields before Burning.* Research Note No. PSW-312. (US Forest Service), 8 pp.

Berrill, M., 1966. Stillness on Eniwetok. *Natural History*, **75**(10): 20 5, 70.

Björnerstedt, R. *et al.*, 1973. *Napalm and Other Incendiary Weapons and All Aspects of Their Possible Use.* (United Nations, New York), 63 pp.

Blix, H., 1974. Current efforts to prohibit the use of certain conventional weapons. *Instant Research on Peace and Violence*, **4**: 21–30.

Blok, P. J., 1907. *History of the People of the Netherlands. IV: Frederick Henry, John deWitt, William III.* [translated from the Dutch by O. A. Bierstadt]. (G. P. Putnam's Sons, New York), 566 pp. + 3 maps.

Blot, W. J. and Miller, R. W., 1973. Mental retardation following *in utero* exposure to the atomic bombs of Hiroshima and Nagasaki. *Radiology*, **106**: 617–9.

Blumenfeld, S. and Meselson, M., 1971. Military value and political implications of the use of riot control agents in warfare. In Alexander, A. S. *et al., Control of Chemical and Biological Weapons*. (Carnegie Endowment for International Peace, New York), 130 pp.: pp. 64–93.

Blumenfeld, S. N., 1966. *Nuclear War and Soil Microflora*. Memo. No. RM-4827-TAB. (Rand Corp., Santa Monica, Cal.), 39 pp.

Blumenthal, R., 1969. U.S. now uses tear gas as routine war weapon. *New York Times* (6 December 1969), p. 3.

Boffey, P. M., 1968. Nerve gas: Dugway accident linked to Utah sheep kill. *Science*, **162**: 1460–4.

Bolt, B. A., 1976. *Nuclear Explosions and Earthquakes: the Parted Veil*. (W. H. Freeman, San Francisco), 309 pp.

Bond, H. (ed.), 1946. *Fire and the Air War*. (National Fire Protection Association International, Boston) 260 pp.

Boucher, G., Ryall, A. and Jones, A. E., 1969. Earthquakes associated with underground nuclear explosions. *J. Geophysical Research*, **74**: 3808–20.

Boyce, J. S., 1961. *Forest Pathology*. 3rd Edn (McGraw-Hill, New York), 572 pp.

Boyle, J. H., 1972. *China and Japan at War, 1937–1945: the Politics of Collaboration*. (Stanford University Press, Stanford, Cal.), 430 pp. + 8 pl.

Brode, H. L., 1968. Review of nuclear weapons effects. *Annual Review of Nuclear Science*, **18**: 153–202.

Brodine, V., Gaspar, P. P. and Pallman, A. J. 1969. Wind from Dugway. *Environment*, **11**(1): 2–9, 40–43.

Broido, A., 1960. Mass fires following nuclear attack. *Bull. Atomic Scientists*, **16**: 409–13.

Broido, A., 1963. Effects of fire on major ecosystems. In Woodwell, G. M. (ed.). *Ecological Effects of Nuclear War*. Publ. No. 917. (Brookhaven National Laboratory, Upton, N.Y.), 72 pp.: pp. 11–19.

Bronson, F. H. and Tiemeier, O. W., 1959. Relationship of precipitation and black-tailed jack rabbit populations in Kansas. *Ecology*, **40**: 194–8.

Brown, A. A. and Davis, K. P., 1973. *Forest Fire: Control and Use*. 2nd Edn (McGraw-Hill, New York), 686 pp.

Brown, F. J., 1968. *Chemical Warfare: a Study in Restraints*. (Princeton University Press, Princeton, N.J.), 355 pp.

Bruner, D. W. and Gillespie, J. H., 1973. *Hagan's Infectious Diseases of Domestic Animals*. 6th Edn (Cornell University Press, Ithaca, N.Y.), 1385 pp.

Buchanan, R. E. and Gibbons, N. E. (eds), 1974. *Bergey's Manual of Determinative Bacteriology*. 8th Edn (Williams & Wilkins, Baltimore), 1246 pp.

Bücherl, W., Buckley, E. E. and Deulofeu, V. (eds), 1968–71. *Venomous Animals and Their Venoms. I and II: Venomous Vertebrates. III: Venomous Invertebrates*. (Academic Press, New York) 3 Vols. (707 + 687 + 537 pp.).

Budowski, G., 1956. Tropical savannas, a sequence of forest felling and repeated burnings. *Turrialba*, **6**(1–2): 23–33.

Budyko, M. I., 1971. *Climate and Life* (translated from Russian; Edited by D. H. Miller). (Academic Press, New York, 1974), 508 pp.

Bugher, J. C., 1951. Mammalian host in yellow fever. In Strode, G. K. (ed.), *Yellow Fever*. (McGraw-Hill, New York), 710 pp.: pp. 299–384.

Bulletin of the Atomic Scientists (ed.) 1960. Biological and chemical warfare: an international symposium. *Bull. Atomic Scientists*, **16**: 226–56.

Burnet, M. and White, D. O., 1972. *Natural History of Infectious Disease*. 4th Edn (Cambridge University Press, Cambridge, England), 278 pp.

Caidin, M., 1960. *The Night Hamburg Died*. (Ballantine, New York), 158 pp.

Caldwell, M. M., 1968. Solar ultraviolet radiation as an ecological factor for alpine plants. *Ecological Monographs*, **38**: 243–68.

Caldwell, M. M., 1971. Solar UV irradiation and the growth and development of higher plants. In Giese, A. C. (ed.), *Photophysiology: Current Topics in Photobiology and Photochemistry*. Vol. 6 (Academic Press, New York), 388 pp.: pp. 131–77.

Canada, 1975. *Suggested Preliminary Approach to Considering the Possibility of Concluding a Convention on the Prohibition of Environmental Modification for Military or Other Hostile Purposes*. Document No. CCD/463. Conference of the Committee on Disarmament, Geneva, 21 + 3 pp.

Cannon, H. W. (ed.), 1971. *Investigation into Electronic Battlefield Program*. US Senate Committee on Armed Services, 221 pp.

Chandler, C. C., Storey, T. G. and Tangren, C. D., 1963. *Prediction of Fire Spread Following Nuclear Explosions*. Research Paper No. PSW-5 (US Forest Service), 110 pp.

Chapline, W. R. and Cooperrider, C. K., 1941. Climate and grazing. In *US Dept. Agriculture Yearbook 1941*, pp. 459–76.

Chern, C. J. and Beutler, E., 1975. Pyridoxal kinase: decreased activity in red blood cells of Afro-americans. *Science*, **187**: 1084–86.

Choquette, L. P. E., 1970. Anthrax. In Davis, J. W., Karstad, L. H. and Trainer, D. O. (eds), *Infectious Diseases of Wild Mammals*. (Iowa State University Press, Ames, Ia.), 421 pp.: pp. 256–66.

Clark, W. H., 1961. Chemical and thermonuclear explosives. *Bull. Atomic Scientists*, **17**: 356–60.

Clarke, R., 1968. *Silent Weapons*. (David McKay, New York), 270 pp.

Cockrell, R. A., 1971. Side effect of tear gas. *BioScience*, **21**: 778.

Cohn, V., 1972. Weather war: a gathering storm. *Washington Post* (2 July 1972), pp. C1–C2.

Commoner, B., 1966. *Science and Survival*. (Viking, New York), 150 pp.

Comroy, H. L., Levy, R., Broce, A. B. and Goldman, L. J., 1971. Prediction of species radiosensitivity. In Bensen, D. W. and Sparrow, A. H. (eds), *Survival of Food Crops and Livestock in the Event of Nuclear War*. Symposium Series No. 24. (US Atomic Energy Commission), 745 pp.: pp. 419–33.

Conard, R. A. *et al.*, 1975. *Twenty-year Review of Medical Findings in a Marshallese Population Accidentally Exposed to Radioactive Fallout*. Publication No. BNL50424. (Brookhaven National Laboratory, Upton, N.Y.), 154 pp.

Conley, C. W., 1967–1968. Great Japanese balloon offensive. *Air Univ. Review*, **19**(2): 68–83.

Cook, R. E., 1971. Mist that rolled into the trenches: chemical escalation in World War I. *Bull. Atomic Scientists*, **27**(1): 34–38.

Cookson, J. and Nottingham, J., 1969. *Survey of Chemical and Biological Warfare*. (Sheed & Ward, London), 376 pp. + 10 pl.

Cooper, C. F., 1961. Ecology of fire. *Scientific American*, **204**(4): 150–6, 158, 160, 207.

Cooper, C. F. and Jolly, W. C., 1969. *Ecological Effects of Weather Modification: A Problem Analysis.* University of Michigan Dept. of Resource Planning and Conservation, Ann Arbor, Mich., 160 pp.

Cooper, C. F. and Jolly, W. C., 1970. Ecological effects of silver iodide and other weather modification agents: a review. *Water Resources Research*, **6**: 88–98.

Craft, T. F., 1964. Effects of nuclear explosions on watersheds. *Amer. Water Works Assn. J.*, **56**: 846–52.

Craven, W. F. and Cate, J. L. (eds), 1950. *The Pacific: Guadalcanal to Saipan, August 1942 to July 1944*, Vol. IV in *Army Air Forces in World War II.* (University of Chicago Press, Chicago), 825 pp. + pl.

Craven, W. F. and Cate, J. L. (eds), 1953. The Pacific: Matterhorn to Nagasaki, June 1944 to August 1945, Vol. V in *Army Air Forces in World War II.* (University of Chicago), 878 pp. + pl.

Cushwa, C. T., 1968. *Fire: a Summary of Literature in the United States from the mid-1920's to 1966.* (US Forest Service SE Forest Experiment Sta.; Asheville, N. Car.), 117 pp.

Cutchis, P., 1974. Stratospheric ozone depletion and solar ultraviolet radiation on earth. *Science*, **184**: 13–19.

Daly, R. A., Manger, G. E. and Clark, S. P. Jr, 1966. Density of rocks. In Clark, S. P. Jr (ed.). *Handbook of Physical Constants.* Rev. Edn Memoir No. 97. (Geological Soc. Amer., New York), 587 pp.: pp. 19–26.

Darcourt, P., 1971. When floods and typhoons hit North Vietnam. *US News and World Report*, **71**(20): 46.

Davis, J. W. and Anderson, R. C. (eds), 1971. *Parasitic Diseases of Wild Mammals.* (Iowa State University Press, Ames, Ia.), 364 pp.

Davis, J. W., Anderson, R. C., Karstad, L. and Trainer, D. O. (eds), 1971. *Infectious and Parasitic Diseases of Wild Birds.* (Iowa State University Press, Ames, Ia.), 344 pp.

Davis, J. W., Karstad, L. H. and Trainer, D. O. (eds), 1970. *Infectious Diseases of Wild Mammals.* (Iowa State University Press, Ames, Ia.), 421 pp.

Dawson, W. L. (ed), 1969. *Environmental Dangers of Open-air Testing of Lethal Chemicals.* Report No. 10. US House of Representatives Committee on Government Operations, 62 pp.

DeBell, D. S. and Ralston, C. W., 1970. Release of nitrogen by burning light forest fuels. *Soil Science Soc. Amer. Proc.*, **34**: 936–8.

Defense Civil Preparedness Agency, US, 1973. *DCPA Attack Environment Manual.* Publ. No. CPG 2-1A1-1A9. US Dept. Defense, 9 chaps [530 pp.].

Deirmendjian, D., 1973. On volcanic and other particulate turbidity anomalies. *Adv. Geophysics*, **16**: 267–296.

Derbes, V. J., 1966. DeMussis and the great plague of 1348: a forgotten episode of bacteriological warfare. *J. Amer. Medical Assn*, **196**: 59–62.

D'Olier, F. *et al.*, 1946. *Effects of Atomic Bombs on Hiroshima and Nagasaki.* Pacific War Report No. 3. US Strategic Bombing Survey, 47 pp. + 2 maps.

D'Olier, F. *et al.*, 1947. *Fire Raids on German Cities.* 2nd Edn European War Report No. 193. US Strategic Bombing Survey, 49 pp. + 17 figs.

Dorn, F., 1974. *Sino–Japanese War, 1937–41: from Marco Polo Bridge to Pearl Harbor.* (Macmillan, New York), 477 pp. + pl.

Dorsman, C., 1947. [Damage to horticultural crops from inundation with seawater.] *Tijdschrift over Plantenziekten*, **53**(3): 65–86, In Dutch.

Duffett, J. (ed.), 1968. *Against the Crime of Silence*, Proceedings of the Russell International

War Crimes Tribunal, Stockholm, Copenhagen. (O'Hare Books, Flanders, N.J.), 662 pp.

Dupuy, T. N. and Hammerman, G. M. (eds), 1973. *Documentary History of Arms Control and Disarmament*. (R. R. Bowker, New York), 629 pp.

Eberhardt, L. L., 1967. *Some Ecological Aspects of Nuclear War*. Report No. TID-23939, US Atomic Energy Commission, 29 pp.

Edvarson, K., 1975. Radioecological aspects of nuclear warfare. *Ambio*, **4**: 209–10.

Eigner, J., 1975. Unshielding the sun: environmental effects. *Environment*, **17**(3): 15–18.

Epstein, W., 1976. *Last Chance: Nuclear Proliferation and Arms Control*. (Free Press, N.Y.), 341 pp.

Epstein, W. *et al.*, 1969. *Chemical and Bacteriological (Biological) Weapons and the Effects of Their Possible Use*. (United Nations, New York), 100 pp.

Ervin, F. R., Glazier, J. B., Aronow, S., Nathan, D., Coleman, R., Avery, N., Shohet, S. and Leeman, C., 1962. Medical consequences of thermonuclear war. I. Human and ecologic effects in Massachusetts of an assumed thermonuclear attack on the United States. *New England J. Medicine*, **266**: 1127–37.

Federal Civil Defense Administration, U.S., 1951. *What You Should Know about Biological Warfare: the Official US Government Booklet*. Publication No. PA-2. US Federal Civil Defense Administration, 32 pp.

Fedorov, E. K., 1975. Disarmament in the field of geophysical weapons. *Scientific World*, **19**(3–4): 49–54.

Fenner, F. and Ratcliffe, F. N., 1965. *Myxomatosis*. (Cambridge University Press, Cambridge, England), 379 pp. + 15 pl. + 1 map + 1 tbl.

Fest, C. and Schmidt, K.-J., 1973. *Chemistry of Organophosphorus Pesticides: Reactivity, Synthesis, Mode of Action, Toxicology*. (Springer, New York), 339 pp.

Fisher, G. J. B., 1946. *Incendiary Warfare*. (McGraw-Hill, New York), 125 pp.

Foister, C. E., 1935. Relation of weather to fungous and bacterial diseases. *Botanical Review*, **1**: 497–516.

Foley, H. M. and Ruderman, M. A., 1973. Stratospheric NO production from past nuclear explosions. *J. Geophysical Research*, **78**: 4441–50.

Fons, W. L., Sauer, F. M. and Pong, W. Y., 1957. *Blast Effects on Forest Stands by Nuclear Weapons*. Techn. Rept No. AFSWP-971. US Forest Service, Div. Fire Research, 104 pp.

Forest Service, US, 1966. *Forest Fire Research: Final Report*, phase I, vol. I. (US Forest Service, Washington). ARPA Order No. 818.

Forest Service, US, 1970. *Forest Fire as a Military Weapon*. (US Forest Service, Washington).

Forman, O. L. and Longacre, D. W., 1969–1970. Fire potential increased by weed killers. *Fire Control Notes*, **31**(3): 11–12.

Fosberg, F. R., 1959 a. Long-term effects of radioactive fallout on plants? *Atoll Research Bull.*, **1959**(61), 11 pp.

Fosberg, F. R., 1959 b. Plants and fall-out. *Nature*, **183**: 1448.

Fothergill, L. D., 1963. Some ecological and epidemiological concepts in antipersonnel biological warfare. *Military Medicine*, **128**: 132–4.

Fowler, E. B. (ed), 1965. *Radioactive Fallout, Soils, Plants, Foods, Man*. (Elsevier, New York), 317 pp.

Fox, G. W., 1970. *Pesticides and Ecosystems*. Literature Search No. 70-39. US National Library of Medicine, 24 pp.

Frankenberg, L. and Sörbo, B., 1973. Formation of cyanide from *o*-chlorobenzylidene malononitrile and its toxicological significance. *Archiv. für Toxikologie*, **31**: 99–108.

Fredriksson, T., 1961. Percutaneous absorption of parathion and paraoxon. IV: Decontamination of human skin from parathion. *Archives Environmental Health*, 3: 185–8.

Freeberne, M., 1973. The land and its people. In Heren, L. *et al. China's Three Thousand Years: the Story of a Great Civilisation.* (Times Newspapers, London), 252 pp. + pl.: pp. 63–102.

Friedman, L. (ed.), 1972. *Law of War: a Documentary History.* (Random House, New York) 2 vols. (1764 pp.).

Fujita, N. and Harrington, J. D., 1961. I bombed the U.S.A. *US Naval Inst. Proc.*, 87(6): 64–9.

Fulbright, J. W. (ed.), 1972. *General Protocol of 1925.* US Senate Committee on Foreign Relations, 439 pp.

Futrell, R. F., Mosely, L. S. and Simpson, A. F., 1961. *United States Air Force in Korea 1950–1953.* (Duell, Sloan & Pearce, New York), 774 pp. + pl.

Giese, A. C. (ed.), 1964–1973. *Photophysiology.* (Academic Press, New York) 8 vols. [2776 pp.].

Gillett, J. D., 1972. *The Mosquito: Its Life, Activities, and Impact on Human Affairs.* (Doubleday, Garden City, N.Y.), 359 pp. + pl.

Glass, B., 1962. Biology of nuclear war. *Amer. Biology Teacher*, 24: 407–25.

Glasstone, S. (ed.), 1964. *Effects of Nuclear Weapons.* Revised edition. US Atomic Energy Commission, 730 pp. + computer.

Gliedman, J., 1972. *Terror from the Sky: North Viet-Nam's Dikes and the U.S. Bombing.* (Vietnam Resource Center, Cambridge, Mass.), 172 pp.

Goldblat, J., 1975. Prohibition of environmental warfare. *Ambio*, 4: 186–90.

Goldblat, J., 1977. Environmental warfare convention: how meaningful is it? *Ambio*, 6: 216–21.

Goldenson, J. and Danner, C. E., 1948. Novel foreign chemical and pyrotechnic munitions. *Chem. and Engin. News*, 26: 1976–78.

Goldsmith, P., Tuck, A. F., Foot, J. S., Simmons, E. L. and Newson, R. L., 1973. Nitrogen oxides, nuclear weapon testing, Concorde and stratospheric ozone. *Nature*, 244: 545–51.

Gooslby, M., 1968. How does nuclear radiation affect honey bees? *Amer. Bee J.*, 108: 352–3.

Goyer, G. G., Grant, L. O. and Henderson, T. J., 1966. Laborarory and field evaluation of Weathercord, a high output cloud seeding device. *J. Applied Meteorology*, 5: 211–6.

Graham, S. A., 1956. Ecology of forest insects. *Annual Rev. Entomology*, 1: 261–280.

Granville, P., 1975 [Perspectives on meteorological and geophysical warfare: a concrete example: the rain-provoking operations in Indochina.] *Défense Nationale*, 31(1): 125–40. In French.

Gravel, M. *et al.* (eds.), 1971–1972. *Pentagon Papers: the Defense Department History of United States Decisionmaking on Vietnam.* (Beacon Press, Boston) 5 vols. (632 + 834 + 746 + 687 + [413] pp.).

Greenberg, D. S., 1972. Vietnam rainmaking: a chronicle of DoD's snowjob. *Science and Govt Rept*, 2(5): 1, 4.

Grimes, A. E., 1972. *Annotated Bibliography on Weather Modification 1960–1969.* Techn. Memo. No. EDS ESIC-1. (US National Oceanic and Atmospheric Administration, Rockville, Md.), 407 pp.

Hachiya, M., 1955. *Hiroshima Diary: the Journal of a Japanese Physician, August 6–September 30, 1945.* Translated from the Japanese and edited by W. Wells. (University of North Carolina Press, Chapel Hill, N. Car.), 238 pp.

Hall, J. A., 1972. *Forest Fuels, prescribed fire, and air quality.* (US Forest Service, Pacific NW Forest and Range Experiment Sta., Portland, Ore.), 44 pp.

Halstead, B. W., 1965–1970. *Poisonous and Venomous Marine Animals of the World. I: Invertebrates. II and III: Vertebrates.* (US Govt Printing Office, Washington) 3 vols. (994 + 1070 + 1006 pp.).

Hampson, J., 1974. Photochemical war on the atmosphere. *Nature,* **250**: 189–91.

Hare, R. C., 1961. Heat effects on living plants. Occasional Paper No. 183. (US Forest Service, S. Forest Experiment Sta., New Orleans), 32 pp.

Hartmann, K., 1967. [Chemical warfare 1966–67.] *Wehrkunde,* **16**: 341–3. In German.

Hartwell, W. V. and Hayes, G. R. Jr, 1965. Respiratory exposure to organic phosphorus insecticides. *Archives Environmental Health,* **11**: 564–8.

Hawley, R. C. and Stickel, P. W., 1948. *Forest Protection.* 2nd Edn (Wiley, New York), 355 pp.

Hayes, W. J. Jr, 1963. *Clinical Handbook on Economic Poisons: Emergency Information for Treating Poisoning.* Publication No. 476. US Public Health Service, 144 pp.

Headley, J. C. and Erickson, E., 1970. *The Pesticide Problem: an Annotated Bibliography.* Research Bull. No. 970. (University of Missouri Agricultural Experiment Sta., Columbia, Mo.), 53 pp.

Health, Education and Welfare, US Dept. of, 1959 a, *Effects of Biological Warfare Agents for use in Readiness Planning.* Emergency Manual Guide No. HEW-2. US Dept. Health, Education and Welfare, 28 pp.

Health, Education and Welfare, US Dept. of, 1959 b. *Effects of Chemical Warfare Agents for use in Readiness Planning.* Emergency Manual Guide No. HEW-3. US Dept. Health, Education and Welfare, 17 pp.

Health, Education and Welfare, US Dept. of, 1959 c. *Effects of Nuclear Weapons for use in Readiness Planning.* Emergency Manual Guide No. HEW-1. US Dept. Health, Education and Welfare, 25 pp.

Heath, R. G., Spann, J. W., Hill, E. F. and Kreitzer, J. F., 1972. *Comparative Dietary Toxicities of Pesticides to Birds.* Special Scientific Report – Wildlife No. 152. US Bureau Sport Fisheries and Wildlife. 57 pp.

Hecht, R., 1976. [Regarding the question of an environmental war.] *Österrechische Militärische Z.,* **14**: 114–115. In German.

Hedén, C.-G., 1967. Defences against biological warfare. *Annual Rev. Microbiology,* **21**: 639–76.

Held, E. E., 1960. Land crabs and fission products at Eniwetok Atoll. *Pacific Science,* **14**: 18–27.

Henahan, J. F., 1974. Nerve-gas controversy: the Army's push for a new chemical weapons system. *Atlantic Monthly,* **234**(3): 52–6.

Heon, N. P., 1964. Flame in war. *Infantry,* **54**(5): 28–32.

Hepting, G. H., 1963. Climate and forest diseases. *Annual Rev. Phytopathology,* **1**: 31–50.

Hersey, J., 1946. *Hiroshima.* (A. A. Knopf, New York), 118 pp.

Hersh, S. M., 1968. *Chemical and Biological Warfare: America's Hidden Arsenal.* (Bobbs-Merrill, Indianapolis), 354 pp.

Hersh, S. [M], 1968–1969. On uncovering the great nerve gas coverup. *Ramparts,* **7**(13): 12–18.

Hersh, S. M., 1972. Rainmaking is used as weapon by U.S. *New York Times* (3 July 1972) 1–2; (4 July) 3; (9 July) E3.

Hess, W. N. (ed.), 1974. *Weather and Climate Modification.* (Wiley, New York), 842 pp.

Hill, J. E., 1961. *Problems of Fire in Nuclear Warfare.* Paper No. P-2414. (Rand Corp., Santa Monica, Cal.), 32 pp.

Hines, N. O., 1962. *Proving Ground: an Account of the Radiobiological Studies in the Pacific, 1946–1961*. (University of Washington Press, Seattle), 366 pp.

Hjertonsson, K., 1973. Study on the prospects of compliance with the Convention on Biological Weapons. *Instant Research on Peace and Violence*, 3: 211–24.

Hodges, J. D. and Pickard, L. S., 1971. Lightning in the ecology of the southern pine beetle. *Dendroctonus frontalis* (Coleoptera: Scolytidae). *Canadian Entomologist*, 103: 44–51.

Holbrook, S. H., 1943. *Burning an Empire: the Story of American Forest Fires*. (Macmillan, New York), 229 pp. + 15 pl.

Holbrook, S. [H.], 1944–1945. First bomb. *New Yorker*, 20(34): 42, 44, 46.

Holifield, C. (ed.), 1959. *Biological and Environmental Effects of Nuclear War. [I.]: Hearings. [II.]: Summary-Analysis*. US Congress Joint Committee on Atomic Energy, 966 + 58 pp. + pl.

Hollister, H. and Eberhardt, L. L., 1965. Problems in estimating the biological consequences of nuclear war (three papers). Report No. TAB-R-5. US Atomic Energy Commission, 40 pp.

Holmberg, B., 1975. Biological aspects of chemical and biological weapons. *Ambio*, 4: 211–5.

Holmes, C. H., 1951. *Grass, Fern, and Savannah Lands of Ceylon, Their Nature and Ecological Significance*. Paper No. 28. (British Imperial Forestry Institute, Oxford), 95 pp. + 7 pl.

Holvey, D. N. *et al.* (eds), 1972. *Merck Manual of Diagnosis and Therapy*. 12th Edn (Merck, Rahway, N.J.), 1964 pp.

Horsfall, J. G. and Dimond, A. E. (eds), 1959–1960. *Plant Pathology: an Advanced Treatise*. (Academic Press, New York) 3 vols. (674 + 715 + 675 pp.).

Horton, A. M., 1975. Weather modification: a pandora's box. *Air Force Mag.*, 58(2): 36–40.

Howard, J. D., 1972. *Herbicides in Support of Counterinsurgency Operations: a Cost-Effectiveness Study*. M.S. Thesis. (US Naval Postgrad. School, Monterey, Cal.), 127 pp.

Hsu Long-hsuen and Chang Ming-kai, 1972. *History of the Sino–Japanese War (1937–1945)*. 2nd Edn. Translated from the Chinese by Wen Ha-hsiung. (Chung Wu Publ. Co., Taipei), 642 pp. + 16 pl. + 47 maps.

Huschke, R. E., 1966. *Simultaneous Flammability of Wildland Fuels in the United States*. (Memo. No. RM-5073-TAB, Rand Corp., Santa Monica, Cal.), 158 pp.

Infield, G. B., 1971. *Disaster at Bari*. (Macmillan, New York), 301 pp. + 16 pl.

Ingersoll, J. M., 1963. *Historical Examples of Ecological Disaster: Engelmann Spruce Beetle; Krakatau*. Report No. HI-243-RR/A2-3. (Hudson Institute, Croton-on-Hudson, N.Y.), 44 pp.

Ingersoll, J. M., 1964–1965. Volcanoes, nuclear explosions and ecology. *Amer. Scholar*, 34: 67–77.

Inglis, D., 1968. Nuclear weapons: the outlook for nuclear explosives. In Calder, N. (ed.), *Unless Peace Comes: a Scientific Forecast of New Weapons*. (Viking, New York), 243 pp.: pp. 43–63.

Ingram, W. M. and Tarzwell, C. M., 1954. *Selected Bibliography of Publications Relating to Undesirable Effects Upon Aquatic Life by Algicides, Insecticides, Weedicides*. Publication No. 400. (US Public Health Service), 28 pp.

Irving, D., 1963. *Destruction of Dresden*. (Wm Kimber, London), 255 pp.

Israelyan, V., 1974. New Soviet initiative on disarmament. *International Affairs*, Moscow, 1974(11): 19–25.

Jackson, W. B., 1969. Survival of rats at Eniwetok Atoll. *Pacific Science*, **23**: 265–75.

Jasani, B. M., 1975. Environmental modifications: new weapons of war? *Ambio*, **4**: 191–8.

Jenkins, D. W., 1963. Defense against insect-disseminated biological warfare agents. *Military Medicine*, **128**: 116–18.

Johnson, F. S., 1973. SSTs, ozone, and skin cancer. *Astronautics and Aeronautics*, **11**(7): 16–21.

Johnston, H. S., 1974 a. Pollution of the stratosphere. *Environmental Conservation*, **1**: 163–76.

Johnston, H. S., 1974 b. Supersonic aircraft and the ozone layer. *Environment and Change*, **2**: 339–50.

Johnston, H. [S.], Whitten, G. and Birks, J., 1973. Effect of nuclear explosions on stratospheric nitric oxide and ozone. *J. Geophysical Research*, **78**: 6107–35.

Jones, G. R. N., 1972. CS and its chemical relatives. *Nature*, **235**: 257–61.

Kanegis, A., 1970–1971. Hidden arsenal: you can't keep a deadly weapon down. *Washington Monthly*, **2**(10): 24–7.

Kantz, A. D., 1971. Measurement of beta dose to vegetation from close-in fallout. In Bensen, D. W. and Sparrow, A. H. (eds), *Survival of Food Crops and Livestock in the Event of Nuclear War*. Symposium Series No. 24. US Atomic Energy Commission, 745 pp.: pp. 56–70.

Kaplan, M. M., 1960. Biological and chemical warfare: communicable diseases and epidemics. *Bull. Atomic Scientists*, **16**: 237–40.

Kaplan, M. [M.], *et al.*, 1970. Health aspects of chemical and biological weapons. (World Health Organization, Geneva), 132 pp.

Karstad, L. H., 1970. Arboviruses. In Davis, J. W., Karstad, L. H. and Trainer, D. O. (eds), *Infectious Diseases of Wild Mammals*. (Iowa State University Press, Ames, Ia.), 421 pp.: pp. 60–7.

Katz, Y. H., 1966. *Nuclear War and Soil Erosion: Some Problems and Prospects*. Memo. No. RM-5203-TAB. (Rand Corp., Santa Monica, Cal.), 87 pp.

Keith, J. O., 1969. [Statement on environmental dangers of organophosphorus insecticides.] In Reuss, H. S. (ed.), *Environmental Dangers of Open-air Testing of Lethal Chemicals*. US House of Representatives Committee on Government Operations, 260 pp.: pp. 99–104.

Kinney, G. F., 1962. *Explosive Shocks in Air*. (Macmillan, New York), 198 pp.

Kipp, D. H., 1931. Wild life in a fire. *Amer. Forests*, **37**: 323–5, 360.

Knight, H., 1966. Loss of nitrogen from the forest floor by burning. *Forestry Chronical*, **42**: 149–52.

Kokatnur, V. R., 1948. Chemical warfare in ancient India. *J. Chemical Education*, **25**: 268–72.

Kolko, G., 1968. Report on the destruction of dikes: Holland 1944–45 and Korea 1953. In Duffett, J. (ed.), *Against the Crime of Silence*. Proceedings of the Russell International War Crimes Tribunal, Stockholm, Copenhagen. (O'Hare Books, Flanders, N.J.), 662 pp.: pp. 224–6.

Kotsch, W. J., 1968. Forecast: change. *U.S. Naval Inst. Proc.*, **94**(1): 69–77.

Kozlowski, T. T. and Ahlgren, C. E. (eds), 1974. *Fire and Ecosystems*. (Academic Press, New York), 542 pp.

Kristoferson, L. (ed.), 1975. Selection of documents . . . pertaining to war and the environment, *Ambio*, **4**: 234–44.

Kudo, R. R., 1966. *Protozoology*. 5th Edn. (C. C. Thomas, Springfield, Ill.), 1174 pp.

Kulp, J. L., 1965. Radionuclides in man from nuclear tests. In Fowler, E. B. (ed.), *Radioactive Fallout, Soils, Plants, Food, Man.* (Elsevier, New York), 317 pp.: pp. 247–84.

Kusterer, D. F., 1966. Application of air-delivered incendiary weapons to limited war in Southeast Asia. Technical Publication No. 4229. (US Naval Ordnance Test Sta., China Lake, Cal.).

Kutger, J. P., 1960–1961. Irregular warfare in transition. *Military Affairs*, **24**: 113–23.

Lacoste, Y., 1972. Bombing the dikes: a geographer's on-the-site analysis. *Nation*, **215**: 298–301.

Lamanna, C., 1959. The most poisonous poison. *Science*, **130**: 763–72.

Lamanna, C., 1961. Immunological aspects of airborne infection: some general considerations of response to inhalation of toxins. *Bacteriological Rev.*, **25**: 323–30.

Lamanna, C. and Carr, C. J., 1967. Botulinal, tetanal, and enterostaphylococcal toxins: a review. *Clinical Pharmacology and Therapeutics*, **8**: 286–332.

Lamb, H. H., 1970. Volcanic dust in the atmosphere: with a chronology and assessment of its meteorological significance. *Phil. Trans. Royal Soc. London*, Ser. A. **266**: 425–533.

Langer, E., 1967. Chemical and biological warfare. I: The research program. II: The weapons and the policies. *Science*, **155**: 174–9, 299–303.

Lapp, R. E., 1958. *Voyage of the Lucky Dragon.* (Harper, New York), 200 pp. + pl.

Larson, C. A., 1970. Ethnic weapons. *Military Rev.*, **50**(11): 3–11.

Lawrence, G. H. M., 1951. *Taxonomy of Vascular Plants.* (Macmillan, New York), 823 pp.

Leitenberg, M., 1967. Biological weapons. *Scientist and Citizen* (now *Environment*), **9**: 153–67.

Levitt, J., 1972. *Responses of Plants to Environmental Stresses.* (Academic Press, New York), 697 pp.

Liebow, A. A., 1965–1966. Encounter with disaster: a medical diary of Hiroshima, 1945. *Yale J. Biology and Medicine*, **38**: 61–239.

Lifton, R. J., 1967. *Death in Life: Survivors of Hiroshima.* (Random House, New York), 594 pp.

Lisella, F. S., Johnson, W. and Lewis, C., 1975–1976. Health aspects of organophosphate insecticide usage. *J. Environmental Health*, **38**: 119–22.

Livingstone, D. A. *et al.*, 1966. Biological aspects of weather modification. *Bull. Ecological Soc. Amer.*, **47**: 39–78.

Lohs, K., 1973. Fire as a means of warfare. *Scientific World*, **17**(1): 18.

Lohs, K.-H., 1974 a. *Chemical Weapons Must be Banned!* (World Federation of Scientific Workers, London), 82 pp.

Lohs, K., 1974 b. [*Synthetic Poisons*]. 4th Edn. Militärverlag der Deutschen Demokratischen Republik, Berlin (DDR) 334 pp. In German.

Lowdermilk, W. C., 1930. Influence of forest litter on run-off, percolation, and erosion. *J. Forestry*, **28**: 474–91.

Lucretius, ca. 55 B.C. On the nature of the universe (translated from the Latin by R. E. Latham, Penguin, Baltimore, 1951), 262 pp.

Lutz, H. J., 1956. *Ecological Effects of Forest Fires in the Interior of Alaska.* Techn. Bull. No. 1133, US Dept. Agriculture, 121 pp.

Lutz, H. J. and Chandler, R. F. Jr, 1946. *Forest Soils.* (Wiley, New York), 514 pp.

MacDonald, G. J. F., 1968. Geophysical warfare: how to wreck the environment. In Calder, N. (ed.), *Unless Peace Comes: a Scientific Forecast of New Weapons.* (Viking Press, New York), 243 pp.; pp. 181–205.

MacDonald, G. J. [F.], 1975–1976. Weather modification as a weapon. *Technology Rev.*, **78**(1–2): 56–63.

Magnuson, W. G. (ed.), 1966. *Weather Modification*. US Senate Comm. on Commerce, 518 pp.

Mahon, G. H. (ed.), 1969. Department of Defense appropriations for 1970, Pt 6, US House of Representatives Comm. on Appropriations, 939 pp.

Manucy, A., 1949. *Artillery Through the Ages: a Short Illustrated History of Cannon, Emphasizing Types Used in America.* History No. 3 of Interpretive Series. US National Park Service, 92 pp.

Marriott, J., 1969. Chemical and biological warfare. *International Defense Review*, **2:** 170–4.

Mason, B. J., 1955. Atomic explosions and the weather. *Weather*, **10:** 139–41.

Mayer, R. L., 1948. Epidemics and bacteriological warfare. *Scientific Monthly*, **67:** 331–7.

McCarthy, R. D., 1969 a. Ban on gas and germ warfare. *US Congressional Record*, **115:** 15763–6.

McCarthy, R. D., 1969 b. *Ultimate Folly: War by Pestilence, Asphyxiation, and Defoliation.* (A. A. Knopf, New York), 176 pp.

McColl, J. G. and Grigal, D. F., 1975. Forest fire: effects on phosphorus movement to lakes. *Science*, **188:** 1109–11.

McConnell, A. F. Jr, 1969–1970. Mission: ranch hand. *Air Univ. Rev.*, **21**(2): 89–94.

McPhee, J., 1973. Curve of binding energy. *New Yorker*, **49**(41): 54–145; (42): 50–108; (43): 60–97. Also 1974 (Farrar, Straus & Giroux, New York), 232 pp.

McQuigg, J. D., 1975. *Economic Impacts of Weather Variability.* (Univ. Missouri, Atmospheric Sciences Dept., Columbia, Mo.), 256 pp.

Meeker, T. A., 1972. Chemical/biological warfare. Classroom Study Series 1(2). (Cal. State Univ. Ctr for the Study of Armament and Disarmament, Los Angeles), 27 pp.

Meinel, A. B. and Meinel, M. P., 1967. Volcanic sunset-glow stratum: origin. *Science*, **155:** 189.

Meselson, M. S., 1970. Chemical and biological weapons. *Scientific Amer.*, **222**(5): 15–25. 148.

Miettinen, J. K., 1974. Chemical arsenal: the time to defuse is now. *Bull. Atomic Scientists*, **30**(7): 37–43.

Mikesh, R. C., 1973. *Japan's World War II Balloon Bomb Attacks on North America.* No. 9 in *Annals of Flight.* (Smithsonian Instn, Washington), 85 pp.

Miles, W. D., 1970. Idea of chemical warfare in modern times. *J. History of Ideas*, **31:** 297–304.

Miller, L. G., 1966. Use of chemicals in stability operations. *Military Rev.*, **46**(12): 43–47.

Miller, R. W., 1974. Late radiation effects: status and needs of epidemiologic research. *Environmental Research*, **8:** 221–33.

Miller, W. L. Jr, 1958. Flame for the infantry. *Infantry*, **48**(3): 65–72.

Mills, J. and Drew, D., 1976. *Serratia marcescens* endocarditis: a regional illness associated with intravenous drug abuse. *Annals Internal Medicine*, **84:** 29–35.

Mitchell, H. H., 1961. *Ecological Problems and Postwar Recuperation: a Preliminary Survey from the Civil Defense Viewpoint.* Research Memo. No. RM-2801-PR. (Rand Corp., Santa Monica, Cal.), 38 pp.

Mitchell, H. H., 1966. Plague in the United States: an assessment of its significance as a problem following a thermonuclear war. Memo. No. RM-4968-TAB. (Rand Corp., Santa Monica, Cal.), 49 pp.

Mitchell, J. M. Jr, 1970. Preliminary evaluation of atmospheric pollution as a cause of the global temperature fluctuation of the past century. In Singer, S. F. (ed.), *Global Effects of Environmental Pollution.* (Springer, New York), 218 pp.: pp. 139–55.

Mobley, H. E., 1974. Fire: its impact on the environment. *J. Forestry*, **72:** 414–17.

Mossdorf, O., 1941. [The war in the far east: the Japanese–Chinese conflict.] (W. Conrad, Leipzig), 300 pp. In German.

Mulla, M. S., Keith, J. O. and Gunther, F. A., 1966. Persistence and biological effects of parathion residues in waterfowl habitats. *J. Economic Entomology*, **59**: 1085–90.

Murphy, J. L., Fritschen, L. J. and Cramer, O. P., 1970. Research looks at air quality and forest burning. *J. Forestry*, **68**: 530–5.

Murphy, P. G. and McCormick, J. F., 1971. Ecological effects of acute beta irradiation from simulated-fallout particles on a natural plant community. In Bensen, D. W. and Sparrow, A. H. (eds), *Survival of Food Crops and Livestock in the Event of Nuclear War*. Symposium Series No. 24. (US Atomic Energy Commission), 745 pp.: pp. 454–81.

Mutch, R. W., 1970. Wildland fires and ecosystems: a hypothesis. *Ecology*, **51**: 1046–51.

Nagai, T., 1951. *We of Nagasaki: the Story of Survivors in an Atomic Wasteland*. (Transl. from the Japanese by I. Shirato and H. B. C. Silverman. Duell, Sloan and Pearce, New York), 189 pp.

National Academy of Sciences *et al.* (eds), 1968. *Postattack Recovery from Nuclear War*. (National Academy of Sciences, Washington), 434 pp.

Neilands, J. B., 1970. Vietnam: progress of the chemical war. *Asian Survey*, **10**: 209–29.

Neilands, J. B., 1972 a. Gas warfare in Vietnam in perspective. In Neilands, J. B. *et al.*, *Harvest of Death*. (Free Press, New York), 304 pp.: pp. 3–101.

Neilands, J. B., 1972 b. Napalm survey. In Browning, F. and Forman, D. (eds), *Wasted Nations*. (Harper & Row, New York), 346 pp.: pp. 26–37.

Neilands, J. B., 1973. Survey of chemical and related weapons. *Naturwissenschaften*, **60**: 177–83.

Neilands, J. B., Orians, G. H., Pfeiffer, E. W., Vennema, A. and Westing, A. H., 1972. *Harvest of Death: Chemical Warfare in Vietnam and Cambodia*. (Free Press, New York), 304 pp.

Nier, A. O. C. *et al.*, 1975. *Long-term Worldwide Effects of Multiple Nuclear-weapons Detonations*. (National Academy of Sciences, Washington), 213 pp.

Nordenskiöld, E., 1918. Palisades and "noxious gases" among the South-American Indians. *Ymer Tidskrift*, **38**: 220–43.

Nordheimer, J., 1975. 29 years after U.S. moved them, Bikini natives sue for safe return. *New York Times* 17 October 1975, 70.

Norman, C., 1973. Binary weapons: death in two parts. *Progressive*, **37**(12): 25–7.

Norman, C., 1974. Pentagon admits Vietnam rainmaking. *Nature*, **249**: 402.

O'Callaghan, T. C., 1973. *Bibliography on Geophysical, Geochemical, and Geological Effects of Nuclear Events*. No. 1 in Bibliographies in Science Series. (General Publishing Services, Alexandra, Va.) 48 pp.

Ognibene, P. J., 1972. Making war with the weather. *New Republic*, **167**(12): 12–14.

Okada, S., Hamilton, H. B., Egami, N., Okajima, S., Russell, W. J. and Takeshita, K. (eds), 1975. Review of thirty years study of Hiroshima and Nagasaki atomic bomb survivors. *J. Radiation Research*, Chiba, **16** (supplement): 1–164.

OKunewick, J. P., 1966. *Effects of Acute Doses of γ-radiation on Pine Trees*. Memo. No. RM-4904-TAB. (Rand Corp., Santa Monica, Cal.), 30 pp.

Osburn, W. S. Jr, 1968. Forecasting long-range ecological recovery from nuclear attack. In National Academy of Sciences *et al.* (eds), *Postattack Recovery from Nuclear War*. (National Academy of Sciences, Washington), 434 pp.: pp. 107–35.

Page, C. H. and Vigoureux, P. (eds), 1974. *International System of Units (SI)*. 3rd edn. Special Publication No. 330. US National Bureau of Standards, 43 pp.

79

Palumbo, R. F., 1962. Recovery of the land plants at Eniwetok Atoll following a nuclear detonation. *Radiation Botany*, 1: 182–9.

Parker, H. M. and Healy, J. W., 1955. Environmental effects of a major reactor disaster. In International Atomic Energy Agency (ed.). *Proceedings of the [First] International Conference on the Peaceful Uses of Atomic Energy*. N.Y.: United Nations Publication No. A/CONF. 8 (United Nations, New York) 17 vols: vol. XIII, pp. 106–9.

Partington, J. R., 1960. *History of Greek Fire and Gunpowder.* (W. Heffer, Cambridge, England), 381 pp. + 3 pl.

Pell, C. (ed.), 1972. *Prohibiting Military Weather Modification.* US Senate Committee on Foreign Relations, 162 pp.

Pell, C., 1973. *Prohibiting Environmental Modification as a Weapon of War.* US Senate Report No. 93–270, 7 pp.

Pell, C. (ed.), 1974. *Weather Modification.* US Senate Committee on Foreign Relations, 123 pp.

Penney, [W. G.], Samuels, D. E. J. and Scorgie, G. C., 1970. Nuclear explosive yields at Hiroshima and Nagasaki. *Phil. Trans. Royal Soc. London*, Series A, 266: 357–424 + 8 pl.

Perry, T. O., 1968. Vietnam: truths of defoliation. *Science*, 160: 601.

Peterkin, F. P., 1972. Chemical warfare: a better alternative. *Marine Corps Gazette*, 56(10): 37–9.

Philpot, C. W. and Mutch, R. W., 1968. *Flammability of Herbicide-treated Guava Foliage.* Research Paper No. INT-54, US Forest Service, 9 pp.

Pimentel, D., 1971. *Ecological Effects of Pesticides on Non-target Species.* (US Office of Science and Technology, Washington), 220 pp.

Platt, R. B., 1963. Ionizing radiation and homeostasis of ecosystems. In Woodwell, G. M. (ed.), *Ecological Effects of Nuclear War*. Publication No. 917 (Brookhaven National Laboratory, Upton, N.Y.), 72 pp.: pp. 39–60.

Pollack, J. B., Toon, O. B., Sagan, C., Summers, A., Baldwin, B. and VanCamp, W., 1976. Volcanic explosions and climatic change: a theoretical assessment. *J. Geophysical Research*, 81: 1071–83.

Popper, R. D. and Lybrand, W. A., 1960. *Inventory of Selected Source Materials Relevant to Integration of Physical and Social Effects of Air Attack.* (Human Sciences Research Publ. No. HSR-RR-60/4-SE, Arlington, Va.).

Porter, D. G., 1972. Bombing the dikes: Nixon's next option. *New Republic*, 166(23): 19–20.

Punte, C. L., Weimer, J. T., Ballard, T. A. and Wilding, J. L., 1962. Toxicological studies on *o*-chlorobenzylidene malononitrile. *Toxicology and Applied Pharmacology*, 4: 656–62.

Purchase, I. F. H. (ed.), 1974. *Mycotoxins.* (Elsevier, Amsterdam), 443 pp.

Purrett, L. A., 1972. Weather modification as a future weapon. *Science News*, 101: 254–5.

Quarantelli, E. L., 1970. Selected annotated bibliography of social science studies on disasters. *American Behavioral Scientist*, 13: 452–6.

Radeleff, R. D., 1970. *Veterinary Toxicology.* 2nd Edn. (Lea & Febiger, Philadelphia), 352 pp.

Ragotzkie, R. A., 1959. Mortality of loggerhead turtle eggs from excessive rainfall. *Ecology*, 40: 303–5.

Rahm, N. M., 1946. Fire fly project. *Fire Control Notes*, 7(2): 4–7.

Randal, J., 1967. Foe's sanctuary hit by fire bombs. *New York Times* (19 January 1967), 1, 3.

Răskovà, H. (ed.), 1971–1972. *Pharmacology and Toxicology of Naturally Occurring Toxins.* (Pergamon, New York) 2 vols. [725 pp. + pl.].

Rayner, J. F., 1957–1958. Studies of disasters and other extreme situations: an annotated selected bibliography. *Human Organization*, **16**(2): 30–40.

Recherche, 1972. [Geophysical warfare makes its discrete debut.] *Recherche*, **3**: 265. In French.

Red Cross, International Committee of the, 1973. *Weapons that May Cause Unnecessary Suffering or Have Indiscriminate Effects.* (International Committee of the Red Cross, Geneva), 72 pp.

Rees, D., 1964. *Korea: the Limited War.* (St. Martin's, New York), 511 pp. + 15 pl.

Reid, G. C., Isaksen, I. S. A., Holzer, T. E. and Crutzen, P. J., 1976. Influence of ancient solar-proton events on the evolution of life. *Nature*, **259**: 177–9.

Reinhold, R., 1972. U.S. attempted to ignite Vietnam forests in '66–67. *New York Times* (21 July 1972), 1–2; (22 July): 5; (23 July): E2.

Reuss, H. S. (ed.), 1969. *Environmental Dangers of Open-air Testing of Lethal Chemicals.* (US House of Representatives Committee on Government Operations), 260 pp.

Rhoads, W. A. and Platt, R. B., 1971. Beta radiation damage to vegetation from close-in fallout from two nuclear detonations. *BioScience*, **21**: 1121–5, 1113.

Rhoads, W. A., Ragsdale, H. L., Platt, R. B. and Romney, E. M., 1971. Radiation doses to vegetation from close-in fallout at Project Schooner. In Bensen, D. W. and Sparrow, A. H. (eds). *Survival of Food Crops and Livestock in the Event of Nuclear War.* Symposium Series No. 24. (US Atomic Energy Commission), 745 pp.: pp. 352–369.

Rickard, W. H. and Shields, L. M., 1963. Early stage in the plant recolonization of a nuclear target area. *Radiation Botany*, **3**: 41–4.

Ritchie, D. J., 1959. Reds may use lightning as weapon. *Missiles and Rockets*, **5**(35): 13–4.

Robinson, J. P., 1973. Binary weapons: a mixed problem. *New Scientist*, **58**: 34–5.

Robinson, J. P., 1974. *Chemical/Biological Warfare: an Introduction and a Bibliography.* Political Issue Series 3(2). (Cal. State Univ. Ctr for the Study of Armament and Disarmament, Los Angeles), 14 + 34 pp.

Robinson, J. P. P., 1975. Special case of chemical and biological weapons. *Bull. Atomic Scientists*, **31**(5): 17–23.

Ronneberg, C. E. *et al.* (eds), 1960. *Nonmilitary Defense: Chemical and Biological Defenses in Perspective.* Advances in Chemistry Series No. 26. (American Chemical Society, Washington), 100 pp.

Rose, H. and Rose, S., 1972. CS gas: an imperialist technology. In Browning, F. and Forman, D. (eds). *Wasted Nations.* (Harper & Row, New York), 346 pp.: pp. 38–49.

Rose, S. (ed), 1969. *CBW: Chemical and Biological Warfare.* (Beacon Press, Boston), 209 pp.

Rosebury, T., 1949. *Peace or Pestilence: Biological Warfare and How to Avoid It.* (McGraw-Hill, New York), 218 pp.

Rosebury, T., 1960. Biological warfare: some historical considerations. *Bull. Atomic Scientists*, **16**: 227–36.

Rosebury, T. and Kabat, E. A., 1947. Bacterial warfare: a critical analysis of the available agents, their possible military applications, and the means for protection against them. *J. Immunology*, **56**: 7–96.

Rosen, M. N., 1971. Botulism. In Davis, J. W., Anderson, R. C., Karstad, L. and Trainer, D. O. (eds). *Infectious and Parasitic Diseases of Wild Birds.* (Iowa State University Press, Ames, Ia), 344 pp.: pp. 100–17.

Rothschild, J. H., 1964. *Tomorrow's Weapons: Chemical and Biological.* (McGraw-Hill, New York), 271 pp.

Ruderman, M. A., 1974. Possible consequences of nearby supernova explosions for atmospheric ozone and terrestrial life. *Science*, **184**: 1079–81.

Runge, E. C. A., 1969–1970. Use weather to predict your corn yields. *Crops and Soil*, **22**(5): 11–13.

Sanford, J. P., 1976. Medical aspects of riot control (harassing) agents. *Ann. Rev. Medicine*, **27**: 421–9.

Sargent, F., II, 1967. Dangerous game: taming the weather. *Scientist and Citizen* (now *Environment*), **9**: 81–8, 96.

Sargent, F., II and Tromp, S. W., 1964. *Survey of Human Biometeorology*. Technical Note No. 65. (World Meteorological Organization, Geneva), 113 pp.

Sauer, C. O., 1950. Grassland climax, fire, and man. *J. Range Mgt*, **3**: 16–21.

Saunders, D. N., 1967. Bari incident. *US Naval Inst. Proc.* **93**(9): 35–9.

Schindler, D. and Toman, J., 1973. *Laws of Armed Conflicts: a Collection of Conventions, Resolutions and Other Documents*. (A. W. Sijthoff, Leiden), 795 pp.

Schneider, M. M., 1976. [Against the military misuse of the environment.] *Deutsche Aussenpolitik*, **21**: 578–601. In German.

Schubert, J. and Lapp, R. E., 1957. *Radiation: What it is and How it Affects You*. (Viking, New York), 314 pp.

Schultz, V., 1966. References on Nevada test site ecological research. *Great Basin Naturalist* **26**(3–4): 79–86.

Schumacher, K., 1970. [Action of chemical warfare agents: symptomatology and therapy.] *Z. f. Ärztliche Fortbildung*, **64**: 97–106. In German.

Scientist and Citizen, (ed.), 1967. Chemical and biological warfare: a special issue. *Scientist and Citizen* (now *Environment*), **9**(7): 111–73.

Scientists' Committee for Radiation Information, 1962. Effects of a 20 megaton bomb. *New Univ. Thought*, **2**(3): 24–33.

Scotto, J., Fears, T. R. and Gori, G. B., 1976. Measurements of ultraviolet radiation in the United States and comparisons with skin cancer data. Publication No. (NIH)76-1029. (US Dept. Health, Education and Welfare), 15 + [202] pp.

Scotto, J., Kopf, A. W. and Urbach, F., 1974. Non-melanoma skin cancer among Caucasians in four areas of the United States. *Cancer*, **34**: 1333–8.

Scoville, H. and Osborn, R., 1970. *Missile Madness*. (Houghton Mifflin, Boston), 77 pp.

Série, C., Andral, L., Lindrec, A. and Neri, P., 1964. [Epidemic of yellow fever in Ethiopia (1960–1962): preliminary observations.] *Bull. World Health Org.*, **30**: 299–319. In French.

Shapiro, C. S., 1974. Effects on humans of world-wide stratospheric fall-out in a nuclear war. *Bull. Peace Proposals*, **5**: 186–90.

Shapley, D., 1972 a. Rainmaking: rumored use over Laos alarms arms experts, scientists. *Science*, **176**: 1216–20.

Shapley, D., 1972 b. Technology in Vietnam: fire storm project fizzled out. *Science*, **177**: 239–41.

Shapley, D., 1974. Weather warfare: Pentagon concedes 7-year Vietnam effort. *Science*, **184**: 1059–61.

Shields, L. M. and Rickard, W. H., 1961. Preliminary evaluation of radiation effects at the Nevada test site. In Bailey, D. L. (ed.), *Recent Advances in Botany*. (University of Toronto Press, Toronto), 1766 pp.: pp. 1387–90.

Shields, L. M. and Wells, P. V., 1962. Effects of nuclear testing on desert vegetation. *Science*, **135**: 38–40.

Shields, L. M. and Wells, P. V., 1963. Recovery of vegetation on atomic target areas at the Nevada test site. In Schultz, V. and Klement, A. W. Jr (eds), *Radioecology*. (Reinhold, New York), 746 pp.: pp. 307–10.

Shields, L. M., Wells, P. V. and Rickard, W. H., 1963. Vegetational recovery on atomic target areas in Nevada. *Ecology*, **44**: 697–705.

Shute, N., 1957. *On the Beach*. (Wm Morrow, New York), 320 pp.

Sidel, V. W. and Goldwyn, R. M., 1966. Chemical and biologic weapons: a primer. *New Engl. J. Medicine*, **274**: 21–7.

Sidell, F. R. and Groff, W. A., 1974. Reactivatibility of cholinesterase inhibited by VX and sarin in man. *Toxicology and Applied Pharmacology*, **27**: 241–52.

Siegmund, O. H. *et al.* (eds), 1973. *Merck Veterinary Manual: a Handbook of Diagnosis and Therapy for the Veterinarian*. 4th Edn. (Merck, Rahway, N. J.), 1600 pp.

Siemes, J. B., 1946–1947. *Report from Hiroshima*. Jesuit Missions, **20**: 30–2.

Simpson, L. L. and Curtis, D. R. (eds), 1971–1974. *Neuropoisons: Their Pathophysiological Actions. I: Poisons of Animal Origin. II: Poisons of Plant Origin*. (Plenum, New York) 2 vols. (361 + 306 pp.).

SIPRI (Stockholm International Peace Research Institute), 1971 a. *Problem of Chemical and Biological Warfare. I: Rise of CB Weapons*. (Almqvist & Wiksell, Stockholm), 395 pp.

SIPRI (Stockholm International Peace Research Institute), 1971 b. *Problem of Chemical and Biological Warfare. IV: CB Disarmament Negotiations, 1920–1970*. (Almqvist & Wiksell, Stockholm), 412 pp.

SIPRI (Stockholm International Peace Research Institute), 1971 c. *Problem of Chemical and Biological Warfare. V: Prevention of CBW*. (Almqvist & Wiksell, Stockholm), 287 pp.

SIPRI (Stockholm International Peace Research Institute), 1971–1975. *Problem of Chemical and Biological Warfare*. (Almqvist & Wiksell, Stockholm) 6 vols. (395 + 420 + 194 + 412 + 287 + 308 pp.).

SIPRI (Stockholm International Peace Research Institute), 1972. *Napalm and Incendiary Weapons: Legal and Humanitarian Aspects*. (Stockholm Intl Peace Research Inst., Stockholm), 125 pp.

SIPRI (Stockholm International Peace Research Institute), 1973 a. *Chemical Disarmament: Some Problems of Verification*. (Almqvist & Wiksell, Stockholm), 184 pp.

SIPRI (Stockholm International Peace Research Institute), 1973 b. *Problem of Chemical and Biological Warfare. II: CB Weapons Today*. (Almqvist & Wiksell, Stockholm), 420 pp.

SIPRI (Stockholm International Peace Research Institute), 1974 a. *Effects of Developments in the Biological and Chemical Sciences on CW Disarmament Negotiations*. (Stockholm Intl Peace Research Inst., Stockholm), 54 pp.

SIPRI (Stockholm International Peace Research Institute), 1974 b. *Offensive Missiles*, Paper No. 5. (Stockholm Intl Peace Research Inst., Stockholm), 34 pp.

SIPRI (Stockholm International Peace Research Institute), 1975 a. *Chemical Disarmament: New Weapons for Old*. (Almqvist & Wiksell, Stockholm), 151 pp.

SIPRI (Stockholm International Peace Research Institute), 1975 b. *Delayed Toxic Effects of Chemical Warfare Agents*. (Almqvist & Wiksell, Stockholm), 60 pp.

SIPRI (Stockholm International Peace Research Institute), 1975 c. *Incendiary Weapons*. (Almqvist & Wiksell, Stockholm), 255 pp. + 12 pl.

SIPRI (Stockholm International Peace Research Institute), 1975 d. *Nuclear Age*. (Almqvist & Wiksell, Stockholm), 148 pp.

SIPRI (Stockholm International Peace Research Institute), 1976 a. *Ecological Consequences of the Second Indochina War*. (Almqvist & Wiksell, Stockholm), 119 pp. + 8 pl.

SIPRI (Stockholm International Peace Research Institute), 1976 b. *Law of War and Dubious Weapons*. (Almqvist & Wiksell, Stockholm), 78 pp.

Slater, W. *et al.*, 1960. *Radioactive Materials in Food and Agriculture.* Atomic Energy Series No. 2. (Food and Agriculture Organization, Rome), 123 pp.

Smedley, A., 1943. *Battle Hymn of China.* (A. A. Knopf, New York), 528 + 16 pp. + 8 pl. + 1 map.

Smith, K. M., 1973. *Textbook of Plant Virus Diseases.* 3rd Edn. (Academic Press, New York), 684 pp.

Smith, L. P., 1970. *Weather and Animal Diseases.* Technical Note No. 113. (World Meteorological Organization, Geneva), 49 pp.

Sorensen, H., 1948–1949. History of flame warfare. *Canad. Army J.*, **2**(4): 16–9; (5–6): 15, 31–2; (7–8): 18–23.

Spalding, J. F. and Holland, L. M., 1971. Species recovery from radiation injury. In Bensen, D. W. and Sparrow, A. H. (eds), *Survival of Food Crops and Livestock in the Event of Nuclear War.* Symposium Series No. 24. (US Atomic Energy Commission), 745 pp.: pp. 245–58.

Sparrow, A. H., Schwemmer, S. S. and Bottino, P. J., 1971. Effects of external gamma radiation from radioactive fallout on plants with special reference to crop production. *Radiation Botany*, **11**: 85–118.

Sparrow, R. C. and Sparrow, A. H., 1965. Relative radiosensitivities of woody and herbaceous spermatophytes. *Science*, **147**: 1449–51.

Spurr, S. H. and Barnes, B. V., 1973. *Forest Ecology.* 2nd Edn. (Ronald Press, New York), 571 pp.

Stearn, E. W. and Stearn, A. E., 1945. *Effect of Smallpox on the Destiny of the Amerindian.* (Bruce Humphries, Boston), 153 pp.

Stecher, P. G. *et al.* (eds), 1968. *Merck Index: an Encyclopedia of Chemicals and Drugs.* 8th Edn. (Merck & Co., Rahway, N.J.), 1713 pp.

Stewart, G. R., 1948. *Fire.* (Random House, New York), 336 pp.

Stewart, O. C., 1956. Fire as the first great force employed by man. In Thomas, W. L. Jr (ed.), *Man's Role in Changing the Face of the Earth.* (University of Chicago Press, Chicago), 1193 pp.: pp. 115–33.

Stickel, P. W. and Marco, H. F., 1936. Forest fire damage studies in the northeast. III: Relation between fire injury and fungal infection. *J. Forestry*, **34**: 420–3.

Stonier, T., 1963. Anticipated biological and environmental effects of detonating a twenty-megaton weapon on Columbus Circle in New York City. *Annals N.Y. Acad. Sciences*, **105**: 291–364.

Stonier, T., 1964. *Nuclear Disaster.* (World, Cleveland), 226 pp.

Strahler, A. N., 1975. *Physical Geography.* 4th Edn. (Wiley, New York), 643 + 39 + 17 pp. + pl. + maps.

Strode, G. K. (ed), 1951. *Yellow Fever.* (McGraw-Hill, New York), 710 pp.

Studer, T. A., 1968–1969. Weather modification in support of military operations. *Air Univ. Rev.*, **20**(6): 44–50.

Sullivan, W., 1975. Ozone depletion seen as a war tool. *New York Times* (28 February 1975), 20.

Taborsky, O. and Thuronyi, G., 1960. Annotated bibliography on weather modification. *Meteorological and Geoastrophysical Abstracts*, **11**: 2181–2415.

Taborsky, O. and Thuronyi, G., 1962. Annotated bibliography on weather modification and microphysics of clouds. *Meteorological and Geoastrophysical Abstracts*, **13**: 702–62.

Takman, J. (ed.), 1967. [*Napalm*]. (Rabén & Sjögren, Stockholm), 189 pp. In Swedish.

Tarr, C. W. Jr, 1965. *Selected Bibliography on CBR Warfare, 1961–1964.* Rev. edn. Publication No. UG 447 (US Library Congress, Legislative Reference Service), 4 pp.

Thomas, A. V. W. and Thomas, A. J. Jr, 1970. *Legal Limits on the Use of Chemical and Biological Weapons*. (S. Methodist University Press, Dallas), 332 pp.

Thomas, R. E., Cohen, J. M. and Bendixen, T. W., 1964. *Pesticides in Soil and Water: an Annotated Bibliography*. Publication No. 999-WP-17. (US Public Health Service), 90 pp.

Thompson, L. M., 1969 a. Weather and technology in the production of corn in the U.S. corn belt. *Agronomy J.*, **61**: 453–6.

Thompson, L. M., 1969 b. Weather and technology in the production of wheat in the United States. *J. Soil and Water Conservation*, **24**: 219–24.

Thompson, L. M., 1970. Weather and technology in the production of soybeans in the central United States. *Agronomy J.*, **62**: 232–6.

Thompson, L. M., 1975. Weather variability, climatic change, and grain production. *Science*, **188**: 535–41.

Thorsson, I., 1975. Disarmament negotiations: what are they doing for the environment? *Ambio*, **4**: 199–202.

Thuronyi, G., 1963. Annotated bibliography on weather modification and microphysics of clouds (supplement). *Meteorological and Geoastrophysical Abstracts*, **14**: 144–244.

Thuronyi, G., 1964. Recent literature on weather and climate modification. *Meteorological and Geoastrophysical Abstracts*, **15**: 1518–53.

Time, 1968. Shrinking sanctuary. *Time*, **91**(17): 28.

Times, The, 1968. *Times Atlas of the World*. Comprehensive edition, 2nd edn. (Times Newspapers, London), 272 pp. + 123 pl.

Todd, O. J., 1942. Taming 'flood dragons' along China's Hwang Ho. *National Geographic Mag.*, **81**: 205–34.

Tucker, R. K. and Crabtree, D. G., 1970. *Handbook of Toxicity of Pesticides to Wildlife*. Resource Publication No. 84. (US Fish and Wildlife Service), 131 pp.

UNSCEAR (United Nations Scientific Committee on the Effects of Atomic Radiation), 1972. *Ionizing Radiation: Levels and Effects*. (United Nations, New York) 2 vols., (447 pp.).

Urbach, F. (ed.), 1969. *Biologic Effects of Ultraviolet Radiation: With Emphasis on the Skin*. (Pergamon, New York), 704 pp. + pl.

Valli, V. J., 1966. *Weather and Plant Diseases: a Review*. Technical Note No. 36-AGMET-3. (US Dept. of Commerce), 24 pp.

VanKampen, K. R., James, L. F., Rasmussen, J., Huffaker, R. H. and Fawcett, M. O., 1969. Organic phosphate poisoning of sheep in Skull Valley, Utah. *J. Amer. Veterinary Medical Assn*, **154**: 623–30.

VanRiper, P. K., 1972. Riot control agents in offensive operations. *Marine Corps Gazette*, **56**(4): 18–23.

Vellodi, M. A. *et al.*, 1968. *Effects of the Possible Use of Nuclear Weapons and the Security and Economic Implications for States of the Acquisition and Further Development of these Weapons*. (United Nations, New York), 76 pp.

Verwey, W. D., 1977. *Riot Control Agents and Herbicides in War: Their Humanitarian, Toxicological, Ecological, Polemological, and Legal Aspects*. (A. W. Sijthoff, Leyden), 377 pp.

Vietnam Newsletter, 1971. Worst flood ever. *Vietnam Bull.*, Washington, **6**(9): 7–9.

Vries, A. de and Kochva, E. (eds.), 1971–1973. *Toxins of Animal and Plant Origin*. (Gordon & Breach, New York) 3 vols. (1107 pp.).

Waggoner, P. E., 1966. Weather modification and the living environment. In Darling, F. F. and Milton, J. P. (eds), *Future Environments of North America.* (Natural History Press, Garden City, N.Y.), 770 pp.: pp. 87–98.

Walker, E. P. *et al.*, 1964. *Mammals of the World.* (Johns Hopkins Press, Baltimore) 3 vols. (1500 + 769 pp.).

Wallace, B., 1973. Conscription at sea. *Saturday Rev. Sciences* (now *Saturday Rev.*), 1(2): 44–5.

Ward, F. P., 1973. *Progress in Ecological Research at Edgewood Arsenal, Maryland: Fiscal Years 1971 and 1972.* Special Publication No. 11 00–13. (US Army Edgewood Arsenal, Aberdeen Proving Ground, Md.), 20 pp.

Wasan, R. P., 1970. Chemical and biological warfare: a select bibliography. *Inst. for Defence Studies and Analyses J.*, 2: 365–78.

Watkins, P., 1966. *War Game.* (Brit. Broadcasting Corpn., London) 16 mm B&W sound film, 47 min.

Watkins, T. F., Cackett, J. C. and Hall, R. G., 1968. *Chemical Warfare, Pyrotechnics and the Fireworks Industry.* (Pergamon, Oxford), 114 pp.

Weast, R. C. (ed.), 1974. *Handbook of Chemistry and Physics.* 55th Edn. (CRC Press, Cleveland), [2279 pp.].

Webber, B., 1975. *Retaliation: Japanese Attacks and Allied Countermeasures on the Pacific Coast in World War II.* (Oregon State University Press, Corvallis, Ore.), 178 pp.

Weiss, E. B., 1974. Weather as a weapon. In Russell, R. B. (ed.), *Air, Water, Earth, Fire: the Impact of the Military on World Environmental Order.* (Intl Series No. 2, Sierra Club, San Francisco), 71 pp.: pp. 51–62.

Weiss, E. B., 1975. Weather control: an instrument for war? *Survival,* 16: 64–8.

Weizsäcker, C. F. von (ed.), 1971. [Results of war and prevention of war.] (Carl Hansen, Munich), 699 pp. In German.

Wells, P. V., 1965. Scarp woodland, transported grassland soils, and concept of grassland climate in the Great Plains region. *Science,* 148: 246–9.

West, C. J., 1919. History of poison gases. *Science,* 49: 412–7.

Westing, A. H., 1973. Postwar visit to Hanoi. *Boston Globe* (23 September 1973), A6.

Westing, A. H., 1974 a. *Herbicides as Weapons: a Bibliography.* Political Issues Series 3(1). (Cal. State Univ. Ctr for the Study of Armament and Disarmament, Los Angeles), 36 pp.

Westing, A. H., 1974 b. Proscription of ecocide: arms control and the environment. *Bull. Atomic Scientists,* 30(1): 24–7.

Wet, C. R. de, 1902. *Three Years War (October 1899–June 1902)* (Translated from the Dutch) (Archibald Constable, Westminster, England), 520 pp. + 1 map.

Wharton, C. H., 1966. Man, fire and wild cattle in north Cambodia. *Proc. Tall Timbers Fire Ecology Conf.*, 5: 23–65.

Wharton, C. H., 1968. Man, fire and wild cattle in Southeast Asia. *Proc. Tall Timbers Fire Ecology Conf.*, 7: 107–67.

Wheat, R. P., Zuckerman, A. and Rantz, L. A., 1951. Infection due to chromobacteria: report of eleven cases. *A.M.A. Archives Internal Medicine* (now *Archives Internal Medicine*), 88: 461–6.

Whicker, F. W. and Fraley, L. Jr, 1974. Effects of ionizing radiation on terrestrial plant communities. *Advances Radiation Biology,* 4: 317–66.

Whittaker, R. H., 1967. Ecological implications of weather modification. In Shaw, R. H. (ed.), *Ground Level Climatology.* Publication No. 86. (American Association for the Advancement of Science, Washington), 395 pp.: pp. 367–84.

Whitten, R. C. and Borucki, W. J., 1975. Possible ozone depletions following nuclear explosions. *Nature*, **257**: 38–9.

Wigner, E. P. *et al.*, 1969. *Civil Defense: Little Harbor Report*. Publication No. TID-24690. (US Atomic Energy Commission), 53 pp.

Wilbur, W. H., 1950. Those Japanese balloons. *Reader's Digest*, **57**(340): 23–6.

Wilford, J. N., 1977. U.S. resettles 75 on Pacific atoll evacuated for bomb tests in 40's. *New York Times* (11 April 1977), 1, 8; (12 April) 3.

Willrich, M. and Taylor, T. B., 1974. *Nuclear Theft: Risks and Safeguards*. (Ballinger, Cambridge, Mass.), 252 pp.

Wilson, J. B. and Russell, K. E., 1964. Isolation of *Bacillus anthracis* from soil stored 60 years. *J. Bacteriology*, **87**: 237–8.

Winters, R. K., 1974. *Forest and Man*. (Vantage Press, New York), 393 pp.

Wolfe, J. N., 1959. *Long-time Ecological Effects of Nuclear War*. Report No. TID-5561. (US Atomic Energy Commission), 5 pp.

Wood, J. W., Johnson, K. G., Omori, Y., Kawamoto, S. and Keehn, R. J., 1967. Mental retardation in children exposed in utero to the atomic bombs in Hiroshima and Nagasaki. *Amer. J. Public Health*, **57**: 1381–90.

Woodwell, G. M. (ed.), 1963. *Ecological Effects of Nuclear War*. Publication No. 917. (Brookhaven National Laboratory, Upton, N.Y.), 72 pp.

Woodwell, G. M., 1967. Radiation and the patterns of nature. *Science*, **156**: 461–70.

Woodwell, G. M., 1970. Effects of pollution on the structure and physiology of ecosystems. *Science*, **168**: 429–33.

Woodwell, G. M. and Holt, B. R., 1971. Effect of nuclear war on the structure and function of natural communities: an appraisal based on experiments with gamma radiation. In Bensen, D. W. and Sparrow, A. H. (eds), *Survival of Food Crops and Livestock in the Event of Nuclear War*. Symposium Series No. 24. (US Atomic Energy Commission), 745 pp.: pp. 482–91.

Woodwell, G. M. and Sparrow, A. H., 1963. Effects of ionizing radiation on ecological systems. In Woodwell, G. M. (ed.), *Ecological Effects of Nuclear War*. Publication No. 917. (Brookhaven National Laboratory, Upton, N.Y.), 72 pp., pp. 20–38.

Wulff, T., Janzon, B., Ohlson, L.-O., Petré, T. and Rybeck, B., 1973. *Conventional Weapons, Their Deployment and Effects from a Humanitarian Aspect: Recommendations for the Modernization of International Law*. (Royal Ministry for Foreign Affairs, Stockholm), 182 pp.

Wurtz, R. H., 1963. War and the living environment. *Nuclear Information* (now *Environment*), **5**(10): 1–20.

York, H., 1970. *Race to Oblivion: a Participant's View of the Arms Race*. (Simon & Schuster, New York), 256 pp.

York, H., 1975. Nuclear "balance of terror" in Europe. *Ambio*, **4**: 203–8.

Related SIPRI publications

Listed below is a selection of recent SIPRI monographs related to the subject of the present text. A wealth of relevant materials is also incorporated in the several *SIPRI Yearbooks*.

1. Nuclear weapons

Near-nuclear Countries and the NPT, 1972, 123 pp.
Nuclear Proliferation Problems, 1974, 312 pp.
French Nuclear Tests in the Atmosphere: the Question of Legality, 1974, 38 pp.
Nuclear Age, 1974, 148 pp.
Safeguards Against Nuclear Proliferation, 1975, 114 pp.
Tactical Nuclear Warfare, 1977. In the press.
Postures for Non-proliferation, to appear in 1978.

2. Chemical and biological weapons

Problem of Chemical and Biological Warfare. I. The Rise of CB Weapons, 1971, 395 pp.
Problem of Chemical and Biological Warfare. II. CB Weapons Today, 1973, 420 pp.
Problem of Chemical and Biological Warfare. III. CBW and the Law of War, 1973, 194 pp.
Problem of Chemical and Biological Warfare. IV. CB Disarmament Negotiations, 1920–1970, 1971, 412 pp.
Problem of Chemical and Biological Warfare. V. The Prevention of CBW, 1971, 287 pp.
Problem of Chemical and Biological Warfare. VI. Technical Aspects of Early Warning and Verification, 1975, 308 pp.
Chemical Disarmament: Some Problems of Verification, 1973, 184 pp.
Chemical Disarmament: New Weapons for Old, 1975, 151 pp.
Effects of Developments in the Biological and Chemical Sciences on CW Disarmament Negotiations, 1974, 54 pp.
Delayed Toxic Effects of Chemical Warfare Agents, 1975, 60 pp.
Medical Protection Against Chemical-warfare Agents, 1976, 166 pp.

3. Geophysical and environmental weapons

Incendiary Weapons, 1975, 255 pp + 12 pl.
Ecological Consequences of the Second Indochina War, 1976, 119 pp + 8 pl.
Law of War and Dubious Weapons, 1976, 78 pp.
Environmental Weapons, to appear in 1978.
Warfare and the Human Environment, to appear in 1978.

Index

90

For Product Safety Concerns and Information please contact our EU
representative GPSR@taylorandfrancis.com
Taylor & Francis Verlag GmbH, Kaufingerstraße 24, 80331 München, Germany

www.ingramcontent.com/pod-product-compliance
Ingram Content Group UK Ltd.
Pitfield, Milton Keynes, MK11 3LW, UK
UKHW021825240425
457818UK00006B/81